The Mediterranean Basin in the World Petroleum Market

PAUL HORSNELL

With :

ALI AISSAOUI
PHILIP BARNES
PETER GREENHALGH
RICHARD HEPWORTH
STEVE MARTIN
KERRY PRESTON

Published by the Oxford University Press
for the Oxford Institute for Energy Studies
2000

Oxford University Press, Great Clarendon Street, Oxford OX2 6DP

Oxford University Press is a department of the University of Oxford.
It furthers the University's objective of excellence in research, scholarship
and education by publishing worldwide in

Oxford New York
Athens Auckland Bangkok Bogotá Buenos Aires Calcutta
Cape Town Chennai Dar es Salaam Delhi Florence Hong Kong
Istanbul Karachi Kuala Lumpur Madrid Melbourne
Mexico City Mumbai Nairobi Paris São Paulo
Singapore Taipei Tokyo Toronto Warsaw
with associated companies in Berlin Ibadan

Oxford is a registered trade mark of Oxford University Press
in the UK and in certain other countries

Published in the United States
by Oxford University Press Inc. New York

British Library Cataloguing in Publication Data
Data Available

Library of Congress Cataloguing in Publication Data
Data Applied for

ISBN 0-19-730021-9

Cover designed by Holbrook Design Oxford Ltd.
Typeset by Philip Armstrong, Sheffield
Printed by Biddles, Guildford

CONTENTS

PREFACE

This book is the result of a project at the Oxford Institute for Energy Studies on the oil market in the Mediterranean. Since its inception in 1982, one of the key areas of research at the Institute has been the study of markets. A series of previous books and papers have covered issues such as the Brent market, the Asian oil market, futures markets and the analysis of futures prices, European oil product markets and informal derivative markets. This study is then an additional thread within that broader patchwork of research.

This book was made possible by the sponsorship of a number of companies, who we wish to thank for their support. The sponsors were the following:

Anadarko
ARCO
BHP Petroleum
Compañia Española de Petroleos (CEPSA)
Deminex
Kuwait Petroleum Corporation
Mobil
Saudi Aramco
Sonatrach
Total
Veba Oel

In addition we wish to thank a number of the benefactor companies of the Oxford Institute for Energy Studies who provided points of contact and commented on the study. These companies were:

BP Amoco
Conoco
Elf Aquitaine
ENI
Enterprise Oil
Mitsubishi
Petroleos de Venezuela

Phillips Petroleum
Repsol
Shell International

A panel was drawn from the above companies, and its members
kindly contributed their time and expertise in providing
comments and information. They are of course not responsible
for any errors, nor do they or their companies necessarily
subscribe to any of the ideas and conclusions of the study.

Liz Bossley (Enterprise Oil), David Beer (Shell), Curtis Brand
(Mobil), F. Cirilli (Agip), Joel Couse (Elf Aquitaine), Christian
Goehr (Deminex), Steven Hewlett (BHP Petroleum), Robert Hill
(Saudi Aramco), Paul Himsworth (Conoco), Suhail Khan
(Petroleos de Venezuela), Mark Lavenstein (Mobil), Antonio
Marin (CEPSA), Shiva McMahon (ARCO), Francisco Moreno
(Repsol), Jean-Marie Peronned (Agip), A. Preuss (Veba Oel),
Lourdes Rodriguez (Repsol), Souad Sadeg (Sonatrach), John
Terroni (Phillips Petroleum), Ichiro Yokose (Mitsubishi), Victor
Zabaneh (Kuwait Petroleum International).

Two workshops were held for study, one in Oxford in
November 1997, and one in Madrid in June 1998. We are
particularly grateful to CEPSA for so generously arranging and
supporting the final Madrid workshop.

We would like to thank Adrian Binks, the Publisher of
Petroleum Argus, for the use of the Petroleum Argus Crude Oil
Deals Database. As in previous studies, we have found the
Petroleum Argus database an invaluable tool for getting
underneath the bonnet of the oil market.

This book is the work of a team of people at the Institute.
The research group for the project comprised Ali Aïssaoui, Philip
Barnes, Peter Greenhalgh, Richard Hepworth, Paul Horsnell,
Kerry Preston and Steven Martin. The text has been primarily
written by Paul Horsnell. In addition, Steve Martin and Philip
Barnes contributed material for sections in Chapter 3, Richard
Hepworth is the principal author of several sections in Chapters
4 and 5, and Peter Greenhalgh contributed material in
Chapter 5.

TABLES

FIGURES

1 A HINGE OF THE WORLD PETROLEUM MARKET

This is a study of the oil market in the countries surrounding the Mediterranean basin. As an objective this requires some justification for the simple reason that, in terms of pure quantities, this is a not a major part of the world petroleum market. As we detail below and in later chapters, the region is small in terms of all the obvious metrics. It contains a small fraction of the world's reserves, and constitutes a similarly small part of production. No Mediterranean country ranks among the world's top ten oil producers. In terms of demand, it emerges as a market of only half the size of the USA or Asia. Oil trading in the region has a small impact on the formation of world prices, the information it carries being swamped by the role played by the North Sea, Rotterdam and New York oil markets.

A small market can still be important if it is highly dynamic, but here too the Mediterranean does not automatically vie for attention. Oil production is static, and oil demand is growing at a rate that is unremarkable compared to other regions. Exploration continues in several countries, but the region absorbs little of the world's expenditure on exploration and development, and attracts little of the journalistic attention paid to more fashionable areas.

The above may imply that the Mediterranean merits little study. However, what makes it of interest has nothing to do with its importance in terms of size or dynamism. The importance comes from pure geography. The Mediterranean represents a part of confluence for four of the world's major current and prospective production areas. Nowhere else in the world, including the US Gulf, are so many producing regions in constant interaction. In that sense it represents one of the hinges of the world market, one of the key areas that binds the system together. Within the basin there is a base load of indigenous production. The overall oil deficit is then balanced by flows into the western Mediterranean from the North Sea and West Africa, into the north-east from Russia, the Caspian and Iraq, and through canal and pipeline via Egypt from Middle East producers.

As the Mediterranean is a relatively small market with little absorptive capacity surrounded by larger and dynamic areas, any external change which affects the area almost inevitably spills out and is transmitted to other parts of the world. The region does not provide any insulation between the major regions, but instead it is a near perfect conductor for any shock. If, for example, Iraqi production varies then that directly impacts on the Mediterranean, leading on to curtailment and diversion of flows from elsewhere.

This chapter provides a quantitative overview of the Mediterranean oil market. As a result of this overview we derive a series of propositions about the nature of that market. Those propositions then form the basis of the remaining chapters, as we detail further below. We describe the system as if it were hydraulic, and so we also quantify the flows within those hydraulics. However, before the market can be quantified, it has to be defined and delineated. If the object of study was, say, Europe, Asia or North America, then that task would be a relatively trivial one. When the region is less well defined, and the Mediterranean cannot a priori be defined at all, then this process requires some justification.

A major problem in any work which seeks to isolate the characteristics of the Mediterranean market, lies in the simple definition and delineation of the region under study. In short, other than as a geographical feature, the Mediterranean as a conceptual feature does not really exist in any other context. There is no unity or strong links in terms of either politics or economics across the Mediterranean. The countries of southern Europe are bonded into northern Europe, and there is little motive to create any meaningful Mediterranean forum. Indeed, to some extent the Mediterranean has become a European protective moat to rival the role once held by the Iron Curtain. In political terms the major trends over the 1990s in the politics of countries north and south of the Mediterranean Sea have been of increased friction, particularly based on often exaggerated European fears about immigration and the export of terrorism.

Before further detailing the propositions we examine in later chapters, it is as well to begin with a definition of what we mean by 'Mediterranean'. We cannot fit into any existing political or economic delineations, simply because there are none of importance in operation. An intuitive definition of the region relies on a general grouping of areas with similar climatic conditions, or in a related way, on the question of how contiguous a country is to the Mediterranean Sea itself. For example, under the intuitive meaning, Switzerland is clearly not a Mediterranean country. We have however based our definition on oil market logistics rather than any political boundaries, and also on the context. Under these definitions, despite the appeals of all intuition, Switzerland most definitely *is* a Mediterranean country. In terms of where it draws its crude oil from, it is orientated towards the south.

We have adopted a definition that produces a partially closed system in terms of oil flows. In considering the downstream and demand issues, we define the Mediterranean as being that area served by oil refineries that source all or most of their crude oil from ports in, or pipelines originating in, the Mediterranean. The details of the area this definition delineates, and an explanation of how pipeline structure produces this area, are given in Chapter 2.

Using our definition, the Mediterranean can be described as a region that, beginning in the south-west of Spain, cuts diagonally across Spain, and then across France before taking in southern Germany, central Europe and the Balkans. From Greece it expands through Turkey and the Levant, before encompassing the entire broad sweep of North Africa. The region comprises 29 countries, with three (Spain, France and Germany) having both a Mediterranean and a northern section. Our basis for ring fencing demand is then drawn from the study of the dynamics of crude oil flows rather than that of climatology. These 29 countries in total constitute a very heterogenous group, covering high, middle and low income countries, areas of high and low population growth, and with a widely differing energy resource allocation and exploitation profile.

In terms of crude oil export flows, the Mediterranean consists of several types of actors. The first of these are indigenous, i.e. countries that adjoin the Mediterranean, amongst which Libya, Egypt, Algeria, Syria and Italy are the main producers. The difference between their production and regional demand is a crude oil deficit which is filled by two types of other countries. The first group we distinguish are those producers for whom pipeline access to ports in the Mediterranean or the Black Sea is a primary or even the only real or potential export method, and those countries who have only limited flexibility in diverting exports out of the Mediterranean. This group then constitutes the countries of the Caspian area, Iraq and also Russia. At one further remove are those countries for whom the Mediterranean market is currently a more minor outlet, or is only occasionally used as a swing outlet, for instance Iran and Saudi Arabia. The distinction between these two latter groups is then that to a large extent the former will normally have first call in filling the Mediterranean deficit, while the latter act more in the role of the equilibrating and marginal suppliers.

Using our refinery flow basis of definition, we have aggregated up from individual country data to produce overall regional figures. For the three countries, France, Germany and Spain that are split by our definition, we have attributed figures in proportion to the percentage of national refining capacity within the Mediterranean area. This proportion is 26.3 per cent for France, 35.1 per cent for Germany, and 85.3 per cent for Spain. Aggregating up from the data of the 29 countries in the region across time, produces the time series for final product demand and crude oil product shown in Table 1.1. Given the long lags involved in the production of data from some of the countries, at time of writing the series can only be created up to 1998.

Table 1.1 demonstrates some of the central features of the

Table 1.1: Mediterranean Refined Product Demand and Crude Oil Production. 1991–8. Thousand Barrels per Day.

Year	Demand	Crude Oil production
1991	8010.9	4568.3
1992	8180.2	4482.5
1993	8139.9	4415.4
1994	8251.3	4461.9
1995	8676.3	4517.7
1996	8789.0	4573.1
1997	9033.3	4566.1
1998	9269.3	4428.1

Source: Own calculations from US Department of Energy World Energy Database

Mediterranean market. First, crude oil production is static with little variation over the course of the 1990s. A key question on the supply side of the market is then whether this torpidity in production is now a set feature, and whether the indigenous Mediterranean producers as a group can expand output, or if their task is merely to manage the path of an irreversible future decline. This issue is taken up further in Chapter 4, but at this point we note that, while the answer to these questions differs sharply across countries, overall the region is not a source of future capacity expansion on any significant scale.

The second key feature of Table 1.1 is that demand in the Mediterranean is expanding, albeit at a very uneven pace. Between 1991 and 1998, an extra 1.25 million barrels per day were added to demand. On a global scale this is not particularly significant; Asian demand can very nearly expand by that amount in a good single year. Within the regional context, however, the increase is significant in that, with static production, all the increased demand has been met by net import flows into the region. Those flows have increased by 40 per cent over the seven years. The evolution of demand and the factors impinging on it are considered further in Chapter 3.

The data can be disaggregated further, as is shown in Table 1.2. At this deeper level of disaggregation, deficiencies in some countries' data mean that 1997 is the last year for which the data can be compiled as of 2000. As the balance is built up from individual country data, import and export figures are gross figures in that they include intra-regional trade. Hence even small net deficits for individual products can mask the presence of a significant level of intra-Mediterranean trade.

All data above the line in Table 1.2 represent refinery inputs, with outputs shown in the lower half. The total figures relate solely to data below the line. Where a refinery output is also used as input in another refinery, for example uncracked fuel oil, vacuum gasoil or naphtha, this is included in the column labelled recycled.

There is clearly some migration of data between categories, most markedly, judging from the figures for unaccounted supply, between LPG and unspecified oil products. However, for crude oil and the main oil products the data appear to be consistent enough to represent a valid snapshot of the regional balance.

Table 1.2: Mediterranean Oil Balance, 1997. Thousand Barrels per Day.

	Production	Refinery Use/Output	Recycled	Imports	Exports	Net Exports	Stock Build	Unaccounted for Supply	Direct Use/Demand
Crude Oil	4566.1	7901.6		6040.0	2712.8	-3327.3	5.8	-14.1	0.2
NGLs	329.0	347.8		22.2	0.3	-21.9	-0.1	0.6	2.6
Other Oils	8.7	413.9	158.5	247.3	9.9	-237.4	-9.3		0.0
Refinery Gain	118.9	118.9							
Gasoline		1731.9		311.4	309.6	-1.8	13.0	22.9	1743.7
Jet Fuel		418.2		71.4	99.0	27.6	8.0	20.2	402.9
Kerosene		103.1		5.2	11.5	6.3	-0.5	-10.6	86.7
Distillate		2757.9		615.6	425.3	-190.3	16.3	-1.4	2930.5
Residual		1877.6		494.2	415.3	-78.9	-21.9	-114.2	1864.1
LPGs		346.3		270.0	216.2	-53.8	4.0	204.4	600.5
Unspecified		1362.9		342.1	345.7	3.6	-12.2	33.4	1404.9
Totals		8597.9		2109.9	1822.6	-287.2	6.5	154.7	9033.3

Source: Own calculations from US Department of Energy World Energy Database

The decomposition in Table 1.2 shows the region's oil deficit to be heavily concentrated in crude oil, with a refined product deficit that is relatively small in terms of the overall level of demand. Of the net oil product imports, about half is used as a refinery input, primarily consisting of uncracked Russian fuel oil. In contrast to the gasoline surplus of northern Europe, the Mediterranean overall is almost exactly balanced.

One factor that sets the Mediterranean apart is the scale of the demand for heavy fuel oil. Throughout most of the OECD, the market for heavy fuel oil has been in long-term decline for over two decades, as it lost share to gas, coal and nuclear energy in its main use in the power generation sector. The most extreme case of this reversal was in the USA, where by 1999 fuel oil represented just 5 per cent of oil demand, and was less than one-eighth of the level of gasoline demand. A similar, but slightly less dramatic, decline has happened in all the countries of northern Europe. By contrast, Table 1.2 shows fuel oil demand to be greater than gasoline demand in the Mediterranean. Without the same degree of indigenous production of gas and coal, and without significant development of nuclear power, the Mediterranean in general did not have the capacity to make the same shifts in power generation as the rest of the OECD. Italy, Spain and Turkey in particular now face making a very late adjustment as the development of the gas market opens up new possibilities for base load power generation.

Table 1.1 implied a total oil deficit in the region of some 4.8 million b/d in 1998. The distribution of this deficit among suppliers to the region can be derived by considering the possible routes into the Mediterranean. In the eastern Mediterranean there are three routes, the first being the pipeline to Ceyhan in Turkey from Iraq, which was inoperative until Iraqi exports resumed at the end of 1997. The pre-Gulf War capacity of the pipeline was 1.6 million b/d, and in 1998 the level of loadings averaged about 0.8 million b/d.

The second route into the Mediterranean is crude oil shipments through the Sumed pipeline to Sidi Kerir, or oil products and crude oil through the Suez Canal. Trade statistics for Sumed and the Suez Canal are shown in Tables 1.3 and 1.4, which provide an overview of the nature of oil trade through these routes.

Table 1.3: Sumed Crude Oil Trade. Suppliers and Destination. 1998. Million Barrels per Day.

Supplier	
Saudi Arabia	1.49
Iran	0.66
Egypt	0.20
Total	2.40
Destination	
Eastern Mediterranean	1.06
Western Mediterranean	0.58
Northwest Europe	0.77

Source: Own calculations from *Middle East Economic Survey*, 24 May 1999

Table 1.4: Suez Canal Oil Trade. 1998. Thousand Barrels per Day.

	South-North	North-South
Crude Oil	332.1	0.0
LPG	99.7	22.2
Gasoline	58.8	9.0
Fuel Oil	50.7	14.8
Gasoil	12.4	1.1
Naphtha	8.8	29.4
Other	17.6	7.2
Total	580.1	83.7

Source: Own calculations from *Middle East Economic Survey*, 12 July 1999

Oil is offloaded at the Ain Sukhna terminal in the Gulf of Suez for transportation through the Sumed pipeline to Sidi Kerir. Table 1.3 shows the origin of crude oil offloaded at Ain Sukhna and the destination of the oil shipped from Sidi Kerir. Total shipments in 1998 amounted to 2.4 million b/d, of which Saudi Arabian crude oil accounted for about 75 per cent. Of these shipments, about 1.65 million b/d stayed in the Mediterranean, while the remainder continued on through the Straits of Gibraltar to northern Europe.

The net flow of oil into the Mediterranean through the Suez

Canal in 1998 amounted to 0.5 million b/d as is shown in Table 1.4. The Suez Canal acts as an important conduit for arbitrage between the European and Asian markets. In that regard, 1998 was an unusual year with Asian demand being depressed by the onset of financial crisis. Total gasoline and gasoil movements south through the canal amounted to just 10 thousand b/d in 1998, whereas the more buoyant condition of Asian demand in 1997 had pulled over 100 thousand b/d south out of the Mediterranean. Indeed, 1998 saw the Mediterranean switch from net exports of gasoil and gasoline through the Suez Canal to net imports.

It is important to note that Suez Canal oil traffic can, as in 1997, comprise simultaneous flows in each direction for oil products. For example, in the case of gasoil Table 1.2 showed the Mediterranean to be a net importer of distillates. However, in years of strong Asian demand it can be a net exporter through the Suez Canal. The key to this apparent contradiction lies in quality differences. What flows south through the Suez Canal is predominantly high sulphur gasoil that does not meet European sulphur limit specifications. It is heading for Asian markets where specifications allow higher sulphur contents. This provides us with a clue that there is a sulphur problem in the refining industry within the region. If, as was the case in 1997, high sulphur gasoil has to make long journeys to find a market, while simultaneously low sulphur gasoil imports are flowing in, there is a strong implication that the structure of the refining industry may be ill suited to the ever tightening specifications in the European market.

The third potential route for ingress into the Mediterranean is from the Black Sea via the narrow and potentially hazardous Bosphorus. In recent years, oil trade through the Bosphorus has averaged 1.4 million barrels per day. The flow is however in both directions. About 1.1 million b/d flows south, primarily representing Russian crude oil, gasoil and fuel oil, but also including a limited volume of Caspian crude oil. A counter flow of slightly less than 0.3 million b/d goes north through the Bosphorus. The latter is comprised of some North African material, but primarily is made up of Iranian oil out of the Sumed pipeline that having loaded at Sidi Kerir carries through to the Black Sea. This then nets out of our flows, being counted as an import into the Mediterranean through Sumed, and then as an export from the region through the Bosphorus.

The fourth and final entry and exit point for the region is through the Straits of Gibraltar, which balances the net position in the eastern Mediterranean. Precision is difficult as we have relied on national trade statistics, and as we have already noted our regional definition cuts across some national borders. However, making assumptions on how to allocate the trade flows in these cases, provides the following characterisation. We estimate the total outflow from the west of the region in 1998 to have been 1.4 million b/d with a matching inflow of 1.4 million barrels per day.

The overall net outflow equates to the imbalance from flows into the east of the region. From the above, the total flows in 1998 from the east through Sumed, the Iraqi pipeline, the Suez Canal and the Bosphorus amounted to about 5.1 million barrels per day. Netting out the reverse flow through the Suez Canal and into the Black Sea brings the net inflow position to 4.8 million barrels per day. The overall regional oil deficit for 1998 implied by Table 1.2 was also 4.8 million b/d, and hence flows through the Straits of Gibraltar must be in rough balance.

The outflow is primarily comprised of Iraqi crude oil, Algerian oil products moving across the Atlantic or into northern Europe, and the crude oil that Table 1.3 shows as moving via the Sumed pipeline into northern Europe. The flow of crude oil exports to the USA from regional producers has been minor over the last decade, even allowing for the sanctions the USA has placed on the major regional producer. The inflow to the western Mediterranean is primarily made out of West African and North Sea crude oil, with the balance being relatively minor flows of Mexican and Venezuelan crude oil, US oil products, and oil products from northern Europe.

The above may seem a complicated mesh of flows and counterflows into the western Mediterranean, however that is precisely the central point. The combined size of the opposing flows amounts to 2.8 million b/d and is again suggestive of some serious dislocations. In terms of crude oil, what enters from the east of the region is predominantly heavy and high sulphur. In the face of a refining structure that does fit the evolution of final product demand, this would produce too much fuel oil and too much high sulphur gasoil. That suggestion seems to be confirmed by the quality of what flows into the west of the region, i.e. light low sulphur West African and North Sea crude oil.

A series of propositions emerge from the quantitative discussion. In the Mediterranean downstream we have suggested that the refining industry has structural problems. Because it has faced a different and more static demand slate compared to the rest of the world, it has evolved in a way that has required little investment. It has been buttressed from developments that have led to more severe restructuring and rationalisation than in northern Europe. In particular, it has until recently been able to produce to less onerous product specifications than the north, and had the support of a large market in heavy fuel oil that has long ceased to be so dominant a feature in other areas. The industry is generally perceived as having severe structural problems, and one of our objectives is to isolate the exact nature of these dislocations. These issues are addressed in Chapter 2. We quantify the differences between Mediterranean refineries and other regions, and provide an explanation of the determinants of refinery closures. From the latter exercise, we derive a ranking of refineries in order of vulnerability to closure. The chapter also traces the path of refinery profitability and the returns to upgraded capacity.

The key issues we address concerning oil demand are primarily those that have the greatest potential for further degradation of the relative position of Mediterranean refining by exacerbating the sector's current weaknesses. This brings in the significant impact of environmental policy, and especially the oil product specification changes originating from the European Commission. This forms a central part of Chapter 3. We have already noted the features of heavy fuel oil demand and gasoil trade in the region. These are expanded in Chapter 3, with a discussion of the future for heavy fuel oil demand, particularly in Italy, and the balance between gasoil and gasoline demand in transportation.

Chapter 4 considers the upstream sectors of the key Mediterranean producers. We have already noted that production has been completely static over the course of the 1990s. We disaggregate this by considering in turn the five main major producers, there being no other country in the region capable of any significant expansion. At the country level we note a more complicated patchwork, with two countries facing seemingly irreversible decline, two managing modest increases, and one struggling to realise its full potential in the face of external political obstacles.

If the regional production profile is unlikely to show major change, that leaves the only possibility of a supply shock in the region as being from proximate producers whose fields are directly linked to the Mediterranean by pipeline, namely the Caspian, Iraq and Russia. Chapter 5 considers the prospects in these countries insofar as they relate to the Mediterranean. Despite the level of hyperbole surrounding Iraq and the Caspian in particular, we find that progress on the ground moves slower than the perceptions of the mind.

Iraq has represented a major source of uncertainty in terms of its production potential, its impact on trade flows and the timing of any resurgence in Iraqi oil given the sanctions regime. However, we can state in advance that we will find reason to doubt any of the more bullish scenarios about Iraq, at least in terms of Iraq's direct impact on the Mediterranean. In 1998, the sharp growth of Iraqi production following the oil for food deal spilled out of the Mediterranean, and was arguably the single most important determinant of the collapse in oil prices in 1998 and early 1999. The lack of demand growth in Asia was a problem, but Asia represented extra demand barrels that did not occur. By contrast, Iraq represented real barrels of supply that could not be contained within the Mediterranean in such an instant surge, and carried on at the margin to bid down the entire structure of world oil prices.

The Caspian represents another source of uncertainty, with, at least *a priori*, both Azerbaijan and Kazakhstan having the theoretical possibility of becoming major exporters. We thus devoted attention to the minutiae of Caspian development, given that the market implications are very directly determined by the progress of a small number of key developments. A crucial question on the supply side is the extent to which the Caspian can match some of the more dramatic expectations that have been raised. Ultimately our conclusions are paradoxical; the Caspian needs to be given attention in order to demonstrate that it does not need much attention within the regional, let alone the global, context.

The final chapter considers the interplay of regional supply and demand as represented by the trading in the region. We have already noted that trading of Mediterranean oil and trading within the region are swamped in size by the main world crude oil and oil product markets. The question then arises as to whether the region is merely a backwater in terms of trading, or whether there is any price formation in the world market that relates to the Mediterranean market. We find that there is an indigenous equilibrating mechanism, namely that represented by the differential between North Sea Brent and Russian Urals for delivery into the Mediterranean.

Russian Urals is a relatively heavy and high sulphur crude oil, whereas most production within the region is light and low sulphur. With Brent related crude oil providing swing into the area, Brent has been the logical metric for the pricing of sales by Mediterranean producers and for other flows into the Mediterranean. It has not always been perfect (as no marker is in perpetuity in all roles), and having the single light sweet North Sea marker did nothing to catch any interplay between north and south Europe. We therefore inspect the nature of the regional spot crude oil market to see if there is any possible basis for a regional light sweet crude oil indicator. However, what we reveal is an extremely thin market, that carries little price information or role in price formation. Chapter 6 also contains some conclusions for the study as a whole.

2   MEDITERRANEAN REFINING

1.   A Definition and an Overview

Refining in the Mediterranean can be readily characterised as a generally low return business, suffering from some chronic deficiencies in its structure as compared to the imperatives of the region's future composition of demand. Those imperatives are the subject of the next chapter, in which we focus on the future of product specifications, the robustness or otherwise of the crucial level of heavy fuel oil demand, and on the balance between gasoil and gasoline in transportation use. In this chapter we seek to (a) diagnose the problem, (b) suggest the desirable order of refinery closures in any rationalisation process, and (c) consider the nature of the signals being sent by the market in the form of refinery profit margins. The chapter has three parts, considering each of these aspects in turn.

We have already noted that the definition of the Mediterranean region can potentially be a slippery concept. Within the context of refining, our definition of what constitutes the Mediterranean uses the flow of crude oil into refineries as the criterion. A Mediterranean refinery is one which takes crude oil out of the Mediterranean, be that by direct pipeline feed from a producing field, by tanker shipment, or through pipelines that originate at Mediterranean ports. This definition does not of course produce an area based on any recognisable political or climatological boundaries. It cuts across three major countries (France, Spain and Germany), and adds some countries which would perhaps not intuitively be thought of as being Mediterranean. However, in terms of regional balances of crude oil flows, this is the only appropriate definition.

While the incorporation of North African and eastern Mediterranean countries into the definition is unproblematic, the division of Europe is based on crude oil pipeline structure. There are four main pipelines that impinge on this division, with schemata for these pipelines being shown in Figure 2.1. Moving east to west, the first of these is the Adria pipeline which originates in Croatia at the port of Rijeka. From Rijeka, spurs of the line enter Serbia, Slovenia, Slovakia and Hungary.

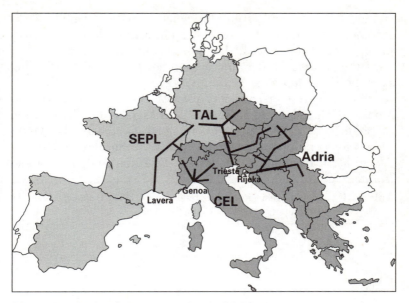

Figure 2.1: Main Mediterranean Crude Oil Pipelines

The latter two countries represent something of a grey area, given that they also have the ability to source oil through the Russian system. Given that the amount of capacity involved is relatively small, we have ignored this complication and included both Hungary and Slovakia.

The second major pipeline is the TAL (Transalpine) line out of Trieste, whose primary route bears north through Austria into southern Germany. Other spurs of the line move oil into the Czech Republic and Slovakia. From Genoa, a set of pipelines known collectively as CEL (Central European Line) move oil around Northern Italy and into southern Switzerland, and until 1996 also pushed into southern Germany. Finally, out of Lavera, the SEPL (Southern European Pipeline System) line moves oil through France into northern Switzerland and southern Germany.

Our allocation of European refineries into the Mediterranean then runs as follows. All of the darker shaded countries in Figure 2.1 are considered Mediterranean, namely Italy, Switzerland, Austria, the Czech Republic, Slovakia, Hungary, all elements of the former Yugoslavia, Albania and Greece. The three lighter shaded countries are split into what can be termed Mediterranean and northern areas. Mediterranean France consists of the coastal refineries at Lavera, Fos and La Mede, together with the three inland refineries fed solely by the SEPL line, namely Reichstett-Vendenheim, Feyzin and Berre l'Etang. Mediterranean Germany consists of the four refineries at Vohburg, Burghausen, Karlsruhe and Ingolstadt. The division of Spain runs from south-west to north-east, with the Mediterranean component being the coastal refineries at Huelva, Algeciras, Cartegena, Castellón de la Plana and Tarragona,

Table 2.1:   Mediterranean Refineries by Country. 2000. Capacity, Number and Share of Regional Capacity.

Country	Capacity Thousand Barrels per Day	Number of Refineries	Per Cent of Regional Capacity
Italy	2340.6	17	25.2
Spain	872.5	7	9.4
France	762.3	6	8.2
Germany	720.3	4	7.8
Turkey	688.2	5	7.4
Egypt	577.8	8	6.2
Algeria	502.7	4	5.4
Greece	382.5	4	4.1
Libya	348.4	3	3.8
Syria	242.1	2	2.6
Croatia	235.0	2	2.5
Hungary	232.0	3	2.5
Israel	220.0	2	2.4
Austria	208.6	1	2.3
Czech Republic	186.0	3	2.0
Serbia	167.3	2	1.8
Morocco	156.6	1	1.7
Switzerland	132.0	2	1.4
Slovakia	115.0	1	1.2
Macedonia	51.2	1	0.6
Lebanon	37.5	2	0.4
Tunisia	34.0	1	0.4
Cyprus	27.0	1	0.3
Albania	26.3	2	0.3
Slovenia	13.5	1	0.1
	9279.4	85	100.0

Source: Own calculations from *Oil and Gas Journal*, 20 December 1999

together with the inland refinery at Puertollano which is fed by pipeline out of Málaga.

Adding in the eastern Mediterranean and North Africa, we arrive at a total number of Mediterranean refineries of 85 spread across 25 countries as shown in Table 2.1, with a total primary distillation capacity of 9.3 mb/d. Regional refining is heavily concentrated, with Italy alone having over one-quarter of total distillation capacity, and the largest five countries (Italy, Spain, France, Turkey and Germany) representing some 60 per cent of capacity.

Breaking the area into sub-regions reveals major quality differences in refining assets. In Table 2.2, we have divided the region into North (western and central Europe), East (primarily the Balkans and the Middle East), and South (i.e. North Africa). We have then classified refineries as complex if they have catalytic cracking or hydrocracking capacity, semi-complex if they have thermal cracking, visbreaking or coking and no complex units, and simple if they have no form of conversion process. The number of refineries in each category is shown in the table by sub-region and by country, with the countries listed in descending order of total crude oil distillation capacity.

From Table 2.2, the Mediterranean emerges as a disparate set of subregions in terms of refining. In the North, simple refineries are in a small minority, representing less than a quarter (10 out of 43) of all refineries. In the East, capacity is less complex, with simple refineries representing 36 per cent (9 out of 25) of the total. In the South, comprised of five countries, four of which have indigenous production of light crude oil, nearly 90 per cent (16 out of 18) of all facilities have no upgrading at all.

The comparative position of the Mediterranean and its subregions on a worldwide basis is shown in Table 2.3, which shows the level of upgrading as a percentage of total distillation capacity. The Mediterranean as a whole is shown to have a level of upgrading only about two-thirds of the world average, with the regional average dragged down sharply by the extremely low level of conversion in the south Mediterranean.

The level of upgrading in the north Mediterranean region is a little lower than in western Europe as a whole. However, the relatively small gap shown in Table 2.3, does not reflect the

---

Table 2.2: Structure of Mediterranean Refining by Sub-Region.2000.
Number of Refineries.

(a) **North Mediterranean**

	Simple	*Semi-Complex*	*Complex*
Italy	3	4	10
Spain	2	-	5
France	1	-	5
Germany	-	1	3
Hungary	2	-	1
Austria	-	-	1
Czech Republic	2	-	1
Switzerland	-	1	1
	10	6	27

(b) **East Mediterranean**

	Simple	*Semi-Complex*	*Complex*
Turkey	1	1	3
Greece	2	-	2
Syria	-	1	1
Israel	-	-	2
Serbia	1	-	1
Croatia	-	-	2
Slovakia	-	-	1
Macedonia	1	-	-
Lebanon	1	-	1
Cyprus	1	-	-
Albania	1	1	-
Slovenia	1	-	-
	9	3	13

(c) **South Mediterranean**

	Simple	*Semi-Complex*	*Complex*
Egypt	7	1	-
Algeria	4	-	-
Libya	3	-	-
Morocco	1	-	1
Tunisia	1	-	-
	16	1	1

Table 2.3: Upgrading by Regions. 1998.

Region	Per Cent Upgrading
North America	39.9
South America	20.1
Western Europe	19.5
Asia Pacific	18.3
North Mediterranean	**18.1**
East Mediterranean	**15.6**
Total Mediterranean	**14.5**
Middle East	13.7
Eastern Europe	7.5
Africa	7.3
South Mediterranean	**0.3**
World Average	21.5

considerably heavier crude oil slate used in the Mediterranean. Were it not for the single factor of a demand barrel weighted towards heavy fuel oil, we would expect the level of Mediterranean upgrading to be significantly above the western European average.

The major deficiencies in Mediterranean refining come not only from a lack of upgrading, but also from a lack of desulphurisation capacity; most of the refineries are short of this capacity, be that hydrorefining or hydrotreating. This has been sustainable up to the present simply due to differing environmental standards. In particular, because Mediterranean product specifications for sulphur content have been less tight than in northern Europe, the majority of refineries have not yet had to make the necessary investments. Should northern and Mediterranean standards start to converge, as is discussed in the next chapter, then desulphurisation represents a major capital expenditure which produces no significant return other than the ability to continue producing.

To illustrate the lack of desulphurisation capacity, we have calculated indices for desulphurisation and conversion capacity relative to distillation capacity for Italy and both the Mediterranean and non-Mediterranean refineries of France, Germany and Spain. For comparison purposes we have also calculated indices for the USA, Japan and the UK. Each of these indices has then been expressed as a proportion of the world average, and the results shown in Figure 2.2.

In Figure 2.2, the origin represents world average desulphurisation and world average complexity. Three very different patterns emerge for Germany, Spain and France. All German refineries sell into markets with tight sulphur specifications, and the southern refineries have little significant ingress for selling off specification material into other markets. As a result, the configuration of German refineries is broadly similar, with both Mediterranean and northern refineries having far above world average desulphurisation, and slightly above average complexity. Spanish refineries differ by complexity, but as they all sell into a market with southern specifications, their level of desulphurisation is the same, and is below world average. In France, all refineries face the same domestic specification, but the Mediterranean refineries have easy access into markets where off domestic specification material can be sold. As Figure 2.2 shows, this results in a dramatic difference. In terms of the level of desulphurisation capacity relative to crude distillation capacity, Mediterranean France is far below the world average, and north France far above.

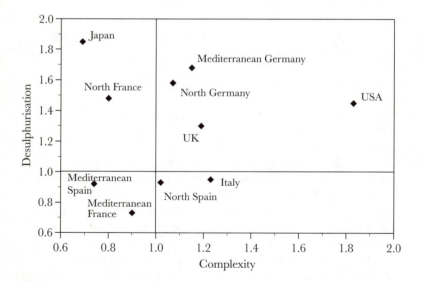

Figure 2.2: Complexity and Desulphurisation Relative to World Average

The three patterns we have for Mediterranean refineries compared to northern refineries in the same countries are then, firstly, similar desulphurisation, similar complexity (Germany), secondly, similar desulphurisation, less conversion (Spain), and finally less desulphurisation and similar conversion (France).

We noted above that the below world average level of conversion capacity in the Mediterranean in general is exacerbated when we make allowance for the relatively heavier crude slate run. That slate is also sourer than average, making the already wide gulf shown in Figure 2.2 in terms of desulphurisation capacity, an even more significant phenomenon.

2. Which Refineries Should Close – The Ranking

Imagine that control of the entire Mediterranean refining industry was passed to a single group of central planners or industry coordinators. They would take the diagnosis of the last section of low average size, low conversion and potentially massively insufficient desulphurisation, and also note the low rates of return and the relatively low rates of utilisation. From that basis, they would swiftly conclude that some urgent rationalisation of the industry was called for.

But how would our planners produce a hit list of refineries with the desired order in which to close them? They could try conventional industry measures, for instance operating margins. The trouble with producing a ranking from this is of course that efficiencies vary as does the possibility for cost saving, so the ranking would reflect how things stand rather than how they might stand. There would also be an information problem, as operational data tend to become rather fuzzy when the providers of that data realise that they will be input to a ranking exercise. The same problems would afflict a rate of return calculation, together with all the accounting problems in deriving the true cost and value of capital. A third solution would be to concentrate on structure, i.e. what configuration and location of refinery is best. The problem here is to know which elements of configuration are actually significant, and the relative weighting for each variable.

In this section we provide a ranking of refineries according to configuration and location variables. We derive the list of significant variables and the weight to be given to each from an analysis of past refinery closures in the Mediterranean market.[1] Closures have been concentrated in the OECD areas of the Mediterranean, with closures elsewhere tending to be the result of acts of war rather than deliberate decision. In addition, for most of our period of study refineries in central Europe and the former Yugoslavia have not been subject to economic decision making. We have therefore confined the analysis to nine countries, namely Austria, Cyprus, Greece, Italy, Switzerland, Turkey and the Mediterranean refineries of France, Spain and Germany as defined in the last section. Our period of study runs from 1976 to 2000.

In 1976 there were 79 operating refineries in the area of study.[2] By 2000, 47 of these were still operating. The bulk of the adjustment in terms of capacity occurred in the early 1980s. From a total of 8.8 million b/d in 1976, capacity had declined gently to 8.7 million b/d in 1981, before plunging to 6.7 million b/d in 1986. Since then, expansion in surviving refineries has partly compensated for further closures. By 2000 the capacity of the refineries under study had reached 6.2 million b/d, exactly the same as in 1990. Indeed, given the generic tendency of reported capacity figures to fail to account fully for capacity creep, the true level of effective rather than nameplate capacity in the Mediterranean areas of OECD Europe is probably now at its highest level since 1986.

We examined the determinants of closure on the sample of refineries in 1976 by using a dummy variable, taking the value of one if the refinery closed and zero if it survived to 2000, in a logit analysis. The variables we used fell in three main categories. The first set were variables relating to the characteristics of the owner(s) of the refinery, the second those relating to the configuration of the refinery, and the third those relating to the location of the refinery. Before presenting the results of the logit analysis and the identification of what are significant determinants of closure within each category, there is also some interest in the variables which were *not* significant.

All variables relating to the ownership of the refinery proved to be insignificant. We found no explanatory power in whether the owner was an integrated company or whether they were one of the majors, the total size of the owner's capacity across

Europe, whether the owner owned one or more refineries, the relative size of the refinery compared to the owner's average size of refinery, or whether the owner was a domestic or foreign concern. In short, there is no evidence that refinery closures have been concentrated among independent firms, and it has not been a process of removing the tail among owners of the small companies. Access to crude oil through integration has made no difference at all. While a producing company or country might buy a refinery to gain integration, closing refineries because of a lack of integration has not been a significant factor.

Among configuration variables there was one major surprise. Size of refinery *per se* is not a significant factor leading to closure. As the average refinery that stayed open was twice the size in 1976 of those that closed, this result needs some explanation. The solution is that larger refineries are more likely to have upgrading, and it is upgrading and not distillation size that is important. In other words larger refineries survived better because they had more upgrading, but being a large simple refinery confers no advantages over a small simple refinery. When upgrading variables were included in the analysis they had all the explanatory power, with distillation capacity size becoming insignificant. Among other insignificant configuration variables were whether the refinery produced lubes, asphalt, hydrogen or any other niche specialities.

Locational variables proved to be important, but several failed to show significance in any formulation of the model. In particular, it made no difference whether the refinery was coastal or whether it was served by a crude oil pipeline, and the distance to the Lavera/Genoa market pricing basis point was also irrelevant.

Table 2.4 shows the seven variables which proved to be significant explanatory variables in the logit analysis, together with the logit statistics. As the dependent variable is a dummy taking the value of one if a refinery closed, a variable with a negative coefficient on a variable is interpreted as being one which made survival more likely. The table shows four significant locational variables. While being close to a crude pipeline made no difference, proximity to a pipeline by which to ship product out did increase the chances of survival. A less important, but still an extremely significant variable, is synergies with petrochemical

Table 2.4: Results of Logit Analysis of Refinery Closures 1976–2000.

	Parameter Estimate	Standard Error	Wald Chi-square	Pr> Chi-square	Standardised Estimate	Odds Ratio
Intercept Term	-0.4025	1.6464	0.0598	0.8068		
Close to Product Pipeline	-2.3824	0.9775	5.9407	0.0148	-0.584	0.092
Petrochemical Synergy	-1.8607	0.8373	4.9382	0.0263	-0.4748	0.156
Cracking Capacity th b/d	-0.1009	0.0421	5.7343	0.0166	-0.6057	0.904
Thermal Cracking Capacity th b/d	-0.1144	0.0596	3.6895	0.0548	-0.3779	0.892
Reforming Capacity th b/d	-0.1153	0.0489	5.5701	0.0183	-0.642	0.891
Country Crude Capacity mb/d	1.3717	0.4814	8.1192	0.0044	1.1245	1
Distance to Nearest Other Refinery	-1.5566	0.6537	5.6693	0.0173	-0.9973	0.211

Refineries predicted Closed	31
of which actually Closed	27
Refineries predicted Open	48
of which actually Open	43
Somer's d	0.859
Gamma	0.86
Tau-a	0.419
c	0.93

facilities. Those refineries feeding petrochemical plants were far more likely to survive. Indeed, about 43 per cent of surviving refineries had some form of petrochemical synergy, as opposed to only 13 per cent of those which closed. Refineries operating in crowded locales were less likely to survive, as is evidenced by the negative coefficient and strong significance of the distance to the nearest other refinery. In other words, some element of market power in the immediate environment has proved to be an advantage. Finally among the location variables, not surprisingly in a declining industry, the greater the total distillation in a country, the greater the propensity of refineries to shut.

Among the large set of configuration variables that were tried, in both absolute and ratio forms, Table 2.4 shows that three proved to be significant. The refineries that survived had more catalytic cracking or hydrocracking capacity, more thermal cracking and more reforming. All other elements of configuration made no difference to survival. Given the results shown, if one had to invest in a single form of capacity expansion in order to improve the chances of survival, then it would be in thermal cracking or reforming, given their larger coefficients and lower per barrel of capacity cost compared to catalytic cracking or hydrocracking. As implied above, the worst form of investment would be in distillation capacity alone which does not in itself affect the propensity to close.

Having highly significant variables does not necessarily imply that the model provides a good explanation of what actually happened. Indeed, in an industry such as refining one might expect to have great difficulty in explaining closure because of the presence of high exit costs. However, the results of the logit shown in Table 2.4 are strikingly good. As noted above, between 1976 and 2000, 32 refineries actually closed and 47 remained open. The model results predict 31 closures and 48 survivals. Of the 31 refineries predicted to close, 27 did in reality. Of the 48 predicted to stay open, 43 did in reality. The model has then erred in 9 cases out of 79, with four refineries predicted to close still operating, and five predicated as having the characteristics of survivors in fact closing. Table 2.5 shows the four refineries that should have closed, and the five refineries that should not have closed. The percentages shown for each refinery are the probability of closure estimated by the model.

Table 2.5:   Refineries Not Fitting Logit Closure Model

(a) Refineries predicted closed that remained operating in 2000

Refinery	Country	Owner	Probability
Mantova-Frassine	Italy	Italiana	93.8
Busalla	Italy	Iplom	81.4
Ingolstadt	Germany	Exxon	62.1
Cremona	Italy	Tamoil	58.0

(b) Refineries predicted open that closed by 2000

Refinery	Country	Owner	Probability
Mannheim	Germany	Wintershall	19.6
Trieste	Italy	Total	27.1
Naples	Italy	Mobil	29.8
Worth	Germany	Mobil	32.0
Rho	Italy	Agip	34.6

Without digressing too far on the special characteristics of the nine refineries shown in Table 2.5, it is worth noting some factors. For instance, among the closures predicted to have stayed open, two were Mobil refineries. Mobil's strategy was generally considered to be both more pan-European and focused on rationalisation retrenchment than that of many other companies.

Having produced an explanation of why refineries have closed or survived, we are now in a position to produce a ranking of which refineries should close first. To do this we have adopted the following procedure. For the 47 refineries that survived into 2000, we have used the 2000 values of the variables that were shown in Table 2.4. We have then calculated the propensity to close on the basis of the 2000 values, and ranked the refineries in descending order as shown in Table 2.6. Thus, the refineries at the top of the list are 'the worst', and those at the bottom are 'the best'. The industry coordinators we began this section with would then close refineries going down the list until enough capacity had been taken off stream.

Our industry coordinators would have to work hard to remove significant capacity from the market. Closing the first five

Table 2.6: 'Worst to Best' Ranking of Refineries Operating in 2000.

Rank (worst=1)	Refinery	Country	Owner/Shareholder	Capacity Thousand Barrels/Day
1	La Spezia	Italy	Arcola	33
2	Busalla	Italy	Iplom	47
3	Tarragona	Spain	Tarragona Asfaltos	21
4	Livorno	Italy	ENI	84
5	Elefsis	Greece	Petrola Hellas	100
6	Collombey	Switzerland	Tamoil	72
7	Frassine	Italy	Italiana Energia	50
8	Ingolstadt	Germany	ExxonMobil	105
9	Milazzo	Italy	ENI/KPC	352
10	Novara	Italy	Sarpom	248
11	Augusta	Italy	ExxonMobil	183
12	Mersin	Turkey	Anadolu	95
13	Batman	Turkey	Tupro	22
14	Thessaloniki	Greece	EKO	67
15	Fos sur Mer	France	ExxonMobil	117
16	Burghausen	Germany	OMV	72
17	Cartagena	Spain	Repsol	120
18	Cressier	Switzerland	Shell	60
19	Kirikkale	Turkey	Tupro	113
20	Berre l'Etang	France	Shell	70
21	Gela, Sicily	Italy	ENI	105
22	Tarragona	Spain	Repsol	180
23	Falconara Marittima	Italy	Api	77
24	Reichstett-Vendenheim	France	CRR	76
25	Castellon de la Plana	Spain	BP	102
26	Priolo,Siracusa	Italy	ENI	220
27	Porto Marghera	Italy	ENI	80
28	Cremona	Italy	Tamoil	90
29	Pantano di Grano	Italy	Raffineria di Roma	82
30	Izmit	Turkey	Tupro	252
31	Taranto	Italy	ENI	84
32	Lavera	France	BP Amoco	200
33	Feyzin	France	Elf	128
34	Aghii Theodori	Greece	Hellas Motor Oil	100
35	La Mede	France	TotalFina	145
36	La Rabida	Spain	CEPSA	100
37	Larnaca	Cyprus	Cyprus Petroleum	27
38	Sannazaro	Italy	ENI	200
39	Aliaga-Izmir	Turkey	Tupro	226
40	Aspropyrgos	Greece	Hellenic	125
41	Puertollano	Spain	Repsol	135
42	Algeciras	Spain	CEPSA	205
43	Priolo Gargallo	Italy	Isab	235
44	Karlsruhe	Germany	OMW	268
45	Schwechat	Austria	OMV	210
46	Sarroch	Italy	Saras	285
47	Vohburg	Germany	Ervin	258

refineries in Table 2.6 only removes 285 thousand b/d of capacity. It is only when the first eleven have been closed that a more respectable 1.3 million b/d disappears. Out of this 1.3 million b/d, over 1 million b/d is in Italy, and none is in France. This then raises the question of why, when it is Italian capacity that should close, that the most talk surrounds French refineries as candidates for closure or divestment. In particular, note BP Amoco's Lavera refinery ranks 32nd on our list, but would perhaps rank well in the top five in terms of past industry and press speculation as well as company strategy.

Of the four refineries in Table 2.5 subject to the vicious suggestion of the model that they should not have been allowed to survive until the present day, the diagnosis has not improved in three cases, with the Busalla refinery second on the hit list, Frassine eighth, and Ingolstadt ninth. Only in the case of Tamoil's Cremona refinery has sufficient investment taken place over the last 22 years to catapult the refinery down the list towards safety.

Several of the refineries shown in Table 2.6 have been part of downstream integration by producing countries. Libyan involvement in Tamoil has produced the investment that as noted above has saved the Cremona plant from failure, but its Swiss operations in the ex-Gatoil plant at Collombey would not appear to be viable in the longer term according to Table 2.6. Saudi Aramco's purchase of the Hellas Motor Oil plant involves a refinery which ranks far down our closure list. Of more significance from the point of view of rationalisation is the purchase by the Kuwait Petroleum Corporation of a stake in the Milazzo refinery, by far the largest in the Mediterranean. Milazzo currently ranks ninth, and is the first sizeable capacity encountered when moving down the list. KPC's involvement, and the significant upgrading of the plant that accompanies it, effectively saves a refinery from closure which perhaps should have closed, and on the basis of what will be its configuration in 2001, it will move far down the list. Put in other words, KPC's involvement means that some other plant than Milazzo that might have survived will now close, unless it receives significant further investment. In particular, if significant capacity is to be removed from Italy, both the Novara and the Augusta plants appear now to be very marginal. Our concentration on Italian refineries comes from two demand side features that are examined at greater length in the next chapter. Italian refineries have survived with low upgrading and low levels of desulphurisation due to a demand slate that has been biased towards heavy fuel oil and low quality product specifications. With the demand for heavy fuel oil concentrated in Italy, should that demand collapse and should environmental specifications tighten sharply, then the Italian refiners will have particular problems. Our contention, explained in the next chapter, is that both these factors will operate.

In our logit analysis, we did not find any significance in desulphurisation as an explanation of exit. This is perhaps not surprising, given that desulphurisation was not a major issue in most Mediterranean countries over the bulk of the 1976 to 2000 period we covered. However, it is arguable that as of now desulphurisation is a major issue, and investment in either desulphurisation or in the additional cost of a greatly sweeter crude oil slate, will represent a requirement for continuing to operate in the industry. Given the alignment of refineries that was shown in Figure 2.2, this suggests that the implications of Table 2.6 might need to be adjusted. In particular, it argues that German and Swiss refineries should be further down the list, and thus would increase the importance of the first seven Italian refineries shown in Table 2.6.

If there is to be a sea change, and the need for desulphurisation capacity becomes critical, then a more *ad hoc* method of ranking is necessary. In Table 2.7 we have shown the configuration of all Italian refineries, ranking them in terms of an upgrading index and in terms of a distillate desulphurisation index. It should be noted that rankings based on such indices may be misleading. As an answer to the old debate about whether it was better to have a large refinery or one with a high percentage upgrading, our analysis above suggests that the answer is neither. It is best to have a refinery that is large in absolute upgrading, but not in distillation size alone. Size does then matter, and so it does not follow that a small but highly upgraded refinery is better than a large one with less percentage, but more absolute upgrading.

The order in which the refineries are listed is a composite drawn from both upgrading and distillate desulphurisation

Table 2.7: Italian Refineries. Upgrading, Hydrorefining and Hydrotreating Capacities.1998. Thousand Barrels per Day. Ranked by Joint Complexity and Distillate Desulphurisation Index.

Company	Refinery	CDU	VDU	Delayed Coking	Thermal Cracking	Vis-Breaking	Cracking- Cat	Cracking- Hydro	Hydrorefining Resid	Hydrorefining HGO	Hydrorefining Dist.	Ref. Feed	Hydrotreating Naphtha	Hydrotreating Dist.	Rank Upgr.	Rank de-S	Rank Logit
ENI	Taranto	84	14	-	27	37	-	16	-	-	34	-	24	-	1	4	4
ENI	Gela	105	53	45	-	-	35	-	-	30	17	17	-	-	3	2	10
Isab	Priolo	235	103	-	33	45	-	65	-	-	-	-	64	96	4	3	2
ENI	Gargallo	77	42	-	19	18	-	-	-	-	40	-	24	-	9	1	9
Italiana	Mantova	50	17	-	8	21	-	-	-	20	-	-	14	-	6	5	14
Saras	Sarroch	285	108	-	-	45	80	50	-	-	-	27	-	76	2	10	1
ENI	Porto Marghera	80	38	-	14	27	-	-	-	-	27	-	16	-	7	7	7
Tamoil	Cremona	90	-	-	-	33	-	6	-	-	27	32	-	-	8	9	6
ENI	Sannazzaro	200	85	-	-	32	34	30	-	-	41	12	27	-	5	13	3
Exxon Mobil	Augusta	183	86	-	-	-	43	-	16	16	-	22	-	40	12	8	11
ENI	Livorno	84	36	-	-	-	-	-	-	-	32	-	22	-	15	6	15
Roma	Rome	82	12	-	-	32	25	-	-	-	21	-	21	-	10	11	5
Sarpom ENI/	Novara	248	27	-	-	-	-	-	-	-	-	-	66	56	14	12	12
KPC	Milazzo	352	79	-	-	-	44	32	-	-	16	-	22	-	11	15	13
ENI	Priolo	220	50	-	-	25	32	-	-	-	18	9	-	-	13	14	8
Iplom	Busalla	47	13	-	-	-	-	-	-	-	-	-	-	-	16=	16=	16
Arcola	La Spezia	33	-	-	-	-	-	-	-	-	-	-	-	-	16=	16=	17

rankings. The rankings shown in Table 2.7 are then inferior to the implied (reverse order) rankings from Table 2.6 (also shown in the last column of Table 2.7), in that they do not include the locational variables which we found to be highly significant, and do not allow for the fine tuning of weights that was possible with the logit. Their only advantage is that they do include a measure for desulphurisation capability. Consideration of de-sulphurisation, according to Table 2.7, among the larger plants still leaves the Novara refinery as having a weak configuration, and again suggests that, from an industry wide perspective, the survival of the Milazzo refinery is not a cause for celebration.

3. Refinery Margins

In this section we briefly consider the market signals being sent to refiners through refinery margins. We first show the simple margin from refining Urals crude oil in Italy, using five cut refinery yields and f.o.b. Mediterranean product prices. This information is shown as a monthly series in Figure 2.3 for the period from January 1986 to December 1999, where the vertical axis is truncated to remove the extreme highs and lows experienced during the Gulf Crisis of 1990–1.

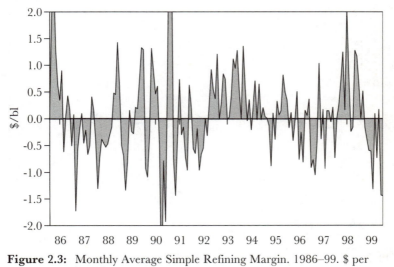

Figure 2.3: Monthly Average Simple Refining Margin. 1986–99. $ per barrel

The simple Urals margin has four main properties. It is low, volatile, seasonal and it shows longer-term cycles. The average of the series shown in Figure 2.3 is just 6 cents per barrel. The series is extremely volatile, the low average masking a standard deviation of 70 cents, even excluding the increased volatility of the Gulf Crisis period. The seasonality of the series is shown in Figure 2.4, which shows average margins by month, and the monthly 90 per cent confidence limits derived from the intra-month volatility. Historically, positive average refinery margins have been concentrated in the fourth quarter of the year, while they have been on average negative in the first quarter, and about zero for the rest of the year. Volatility is relatively low in the second and third quarters, and at its highest in the first quarter.

The normal seasonal pattern can then be characterised as a period of uneventful doldrums lasting from May through to September, followed by a period in October and November in which the probability of positive margins is at its highest. The volatility then increases sharply in the period through to April, during which margins can be either at their absolute highest or their lowest. The suggestion can be made then that the northern European seasonality of demand, driven primarily by the severity

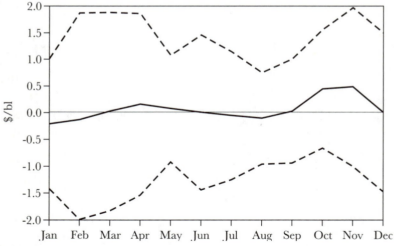

Figure 2.4:   Average Monthly Simple Refining Margin, and 90 per cent Confidence Intervals

of the winter and the strength of distillate demand, also finds its reflection in Mediterranean refining margins, regardless of the lower seasonality of Mediterranean demand.

Because of the presence of strong volatility and seasonality, Figure 2.3 disguises the presence of any longer-term cycle. Such a cycle is revealed by taking annual averages as shown in Figure 2.5. After strong margins were achieved in 1993, profitability from straight run refining declined in each of the next four years. In total, this decline reduced the level of the margin a full 80 cents per barrel. After this decline, 1998 proved to be the best year for refining margins over the period, and 1999 proved to be the worst with margins becoming deeply negative.

The varying fortunes in 1998 and in 1999 are in fact connected, and indeed to a large extent the poor margins of 1999 are due to the strong margins of 1998. The oil market in 1998 was characterised by an excess of crude oil supply, brought about by the return of Iraq to world markets from the end of 1997 and the increase in OPEC production following the OPEC meeting of November 1997. With all the weakness concentrated on crude oil, refinery margins strengthened. An incentive was created to run at full capacity, and the development of a contango in the time structure of prices, i.e. a premium for

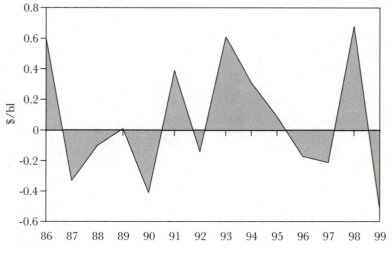

Figure 2.5: Average Annual Simple Refining Margin. 1986–99. $ per barrel

future delivery dates, created a power incentive to put oil products into storage. When, in early 1999, OPEC members and other producers took action, they had only a blunt weapon to use. The problem of the oil market had become a massive excess of inventories, and that excess was heavily concentrated in oil products. The producers' only available correction mechanism was the supply of crude oil. Hence, for adjustment to work the mechanism was to tighten the crude oil market, thus reduce refinery margins and refinery utilisation rates, and encourage the drawing down of inventories. To that extent, poor refining margins in 1999 were the direct aftermath of the conditions created by the good margins of the previous year.

Despite the upwards blip in 1998, overall refining profits in the Mediterranean were under pressure throughout the 1990s, and particularly in the latter half of the decade. The first market signal being sent through refinery margins then appears to be a straightforward message that there is overcapacity in the system.

Turning to the margins for conversion capacity, Figure 2.6 shows the upgrading margin, i.e. the difference between the margin from upgraded capacity and that from straight run refining, as a monthly series, and Figure 2.7 shows it as an annual series. After the Gulf crisis induced the high margins of 1990–1, the return to upgrading fell consistently towards a low

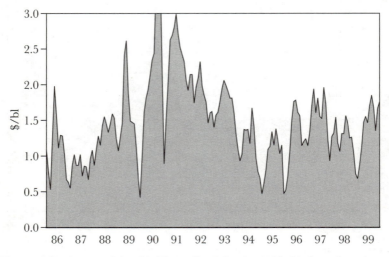

Figure 2.6: Average Monthly Upgrading Margin. 1986–99. $ per barrel

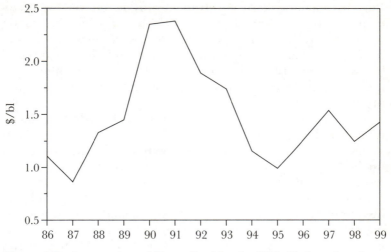

Figure 2.7: Average Annual Upgrading Margin. 1986–99. $ per barrel

in 1995, by which time the upgrading margin had lost $1.40 per barrel of its value. The cycle then turned in 1996, with a 60 cent per barrel recovery by 1997 from the low.

While the effects of the general overexpansion in cracking capacity in the early 1990s are beginning to work out of the system, current margins still do not represent a strong enough market signal to invest in further upgrading capacity. In large part the linkages between Rotterdam and Mediterranean product prices are strong enough to mean that the over-investment in upgrading in northern Europe is now discouraging investment in the south. One solution is then to consider a conversion margin that is primarily determined by local conditions and not by Rotterdam, namely the spread between fuel oil and electricity. This brings us to gasification, which given current relative prices and other incentives, has started to become a significant form of upgrading carried out in Mediterranean refineries. Gasification projects to date have been concentrated in Europe, and most particularly in Italy and Spain. A series of investments have already been made, for instance in Italy the Sarroch refinery has a 550 MW integrated gasification combined-cycle plant, and the Priolo Gargallo refinery has a 512 MW unit. Admittedly the economics of such projects in

Italy are encouraged by government subsidy, but the electricity to fuel oil spread is attractive in itself. However, while gasification is the only available technical fix which solves many aspects of the fundamental problem of Mediterranean refining as expressed below, the scale of plant achievable under current technology is not sufficient to make significant inroads into the fuel oil surplus problem.

We can summarise the major problem for Mediterranean refining as being how to reduce yields of heavy fuel oil, without adding to gasoil and gasoline production, and thus incurring further costs in bringing those lighter products up to the tightening specifications. The northern European refiner by contrast has fewer concerns with fuel oil yields, and less investment to make to meet specifications, and their problem is mainly one of the quality of conversion, and in particular the gasoline surplus versus the gasoil deficit. The Mediterranean problem is then the more serious. Under current conditions, just about the most undesirable position to be in is to be fuel oil long, sulphur long, and octane and quality short. That is precisely the position where the Mediterranean industry currently is, and the next chapter suggests that demand trends will only compound those problems.

Notes

1.   The following analysis builds on work undertaken in Robert Bacon, 'The Propensity of European Refineries to shut between 1976 and 1986' in Robert Bacon et al. (1990), *Demand, Prices and the Refining Industry*, Oxford University Press for the Oxford Institute for Energy Studies. It differs in the following respects. We have confined the analysis solely to Mediterranean refineries, and expanded the end point of study from 1976 to 2000. We have also used a different statistical tool, logit analysis, rather than the probit and linear probability models estimated by Bacon.

2.   In a few cases, solely in Germany, there have been refinery mergers rather than straightforward shut-down. As the number is small, and accounting for mergers separately greatly complicates the econometrics of the problem, we have treated these German refineries as if they had already merged at the start of the period.

3 ISSUES IN MEDITERRANEAN OIL DEMAND

1. Introduction

In the previous chapter we identified two main issues from the demand side of the market which impinge strongly on the refinery economics of the Mediterranean. First, the region has a shortage of desulphurisation capacity, leaving scope for dislocation and considerable expense should the environmental specifications for oil products tighten. Secondly, the region does not have an abundance of conversion capacity, and is operating with a below world average level of upgrading despite having a heavier than average crude oil slate. This has been sustainable due to the relatively high level of heavy fuel oil demand, primarily led by power generation in Italy. The overall balance of the region is then particularly sensitive to the robustness of that demand. Should heavy fuel oil demand drop precipitously in the face of an acceleration of the penetration of natural gas, the dislocations caused would be considerable.

We cover the two main demand issues noted above in sections 3 and 4. In section 2 we add a further European issue. While the situation (in terms of quantity if not quality) is less severe in the Mediterranean than in northern Europe, overall Europe is long on gasoline production and short of middle distillate production. We focus in this analysis on one key determinant of the imbalance, namely the division of transport demand between gasoline and diesel. The final section of this chapter contains an overview of Mediterranean demand patterns, and provides some metrics on their evolution.

2. The Gasoline and Diesel Balance

While northern Europe has experienced a large gasoline surplus combined with a gasoil deficit, the problem in the Mediterranean has been different. As was shown in Table 1.2, gasoline is more or less in balance for the region as a whole, with there being a very slight deficit. The regional differences are again attributable to one of the structural features of Mediterranean refining, i.e. that investment takes place at a slower rate than in the north, and normally to a lesser final extent. The northern gasoline surplus was in large part an artefact of over-investment in catalytic crackers that happened to coincide with a period when average crude oil production became considerably lighter. A relative lack of investment in the Mediterranean on one hand proved to be highly beneficial in that it prevented a large structural gasoline surplus. However, in avoiding the quantity problem, a quality problem was created. With the slow take-up of unleaded fuel in the Mediterranean, reforming capacity has been slow to expand. As a result, refiners have found themselves to be slightly long in quantity, but severely short in octane. While a boost in gasoline demand relative to automotive gasoil would unambiguously improve the overall balance in the north, in the Mediterranean any increase, particularly if biased towards unleaded would quickly remove the quantity surplus, but exacerbate the quality deficit.

Like northern Europe, the Mediterranean has had a tendency towards gasoil deficit. However, again the quality aspects overwhelm the quantity concerns. As we saw in the last chapter, the Mediterranean refining system is short of desulphurisation capacity. Thus, the overall deficit has coexisted with a surplus of material that does meet the 0.05 per cent EU sulphur specification, giving rise to a significant quality trade.

For northern European markets the question of the relative growth of gasoline and automotive gasoil demand is simply one of whether the current structural deficits will widen or narrow. The issue is black and white, in that gasoline growth is good, and gasoil growth is bad. No such easy division exists in the Mediterranean market, where the question simply provides the answer as to which quality deficit will widen most, i.e. whether the greatest problem will be the pressure on reforming or on desulphurisation capacity. In this section we try to answer the question as to whether the growth of automotive gasoil demand will continue to be strong or whether it will abate, and what factors are determining the process.

The strong growth in the use of automotive gasoil since the 1970s has been a significant phenomenon at the aggregate European level. Within OECD Europe as a whole, transport sector demand for gasoil rose from 51 million tonnes in 1973 to 122 million tonnes in 1995, with transport now accounting for some 55 per cent of all gasoil use, as opposed to under 25 per cent in 1973. This strong growth in the use of automotive gasoil represents one of the major differences between the structure of demand in Europe and that in the USA. By 1995, gasoil represented just 19 per cent of combined US gasoline and gasoil use in transport, compared to 47 per cent in Europe. In Europe, gasoil dominates in heavy goods vehicles, and takes a significant share of the car stock. In the USA, there is a greater proportion of heavy duty gasoline vehicles, and gasoil has made little impact as a car fuel. Sales of diesel cars increased after the second oil price shock of 1979, peaking two years later at approximately 5 per cent of new car purchases. However, sales have since returned to the low pre-1970 levels, as a result of problems with consumer acceptance and because the price advantage of diesel which, during the early 1980s was cheaper than gasoline, has declined and reversed.

In Europe, automotive gasoil was regarded by some governments as a way of improving oil security and their trade balances. Motorists were attracted by the prospect of cheaper fuel and by greater fuel economy associated with diesel cars. Meanwhile, oil companies which, in the early 1980s, were facing declining residential and industrial demand for gasoil welcomed a new outlet for the fuel. For car manufacturers, the diesel model represented a new market segment and therefore a new source of increased sales of cars, which rested comfortably alongside the well-established fuelling network.

The move towards gasoil has accelerated in the 1990s, with consumption within the transport sector growing at annual rates of between 3 and 5 per cent. Within this growth, the most significant shifts to gasoil have occurred in Mediterranean countries, and in particular France and Spain. Figure 3.1 shows the proportion of diesel passenger cars in the composition of sales of new passenger vehicles for selected countries.

As Figure 3.1 shows, diesel cars have found their largest market in France. In 1994 and 1995, close to 50 per cent of all new car sales in this country were diesel models, although this share dropped below 40 per cent in 1996. The importance of diesel cars in France reflects strong government support for diesel, as part of its general strategy to minimise oil use. Diesel cars have been promoted by tax incentives, both on the purchase

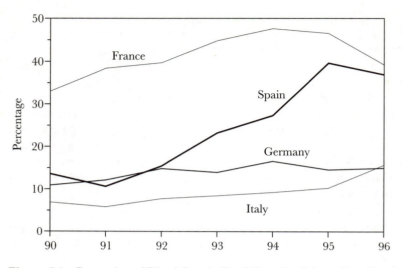

Figure 3.1:   Proportion of Diesel Cars in Total New Car Sales. selected
Countries. 1990–96

of cars (the vehicle purchase tax on diesel cars has traditionally
been lower than that on gasoline models), and in terms of the
tax differential between diesel and gasoline (discussed in more
detail in a subsequent section), which has helped to maintain a
strong price advantage for diesel vis-à-vis gasoline. Moreover,
the national automotive industry is keen to promote diesel-
powered vehicles. The French car industry has emerged as a
major exporter of diesel cars, and is a prominent supplier of
diesel engines to other car makers. The drop in diesel's share in
1996 can be attributed to growing concern about the
environmental consequences of diesel emissions (discussed below)
and the expectation that diesel's fiscal advantage may be reduced
as part of the national ecology tax under discussion in France.

The greatest growth in the importance of diesel over the
1990s has occurred in Spain. From less than 15 per cent at the
beginning of the decade, the popularity of diesel cars has grown
to the point where they accounted for 37 per cent of new car
sales in 1996. The other countries featured in Figure 3.1 have
not embraced diesel vehicles with quite the same enthusiasm as
the French and Spanish. In Germany and Italy the share of
total sales accounted for by diesel cars has shown a slower

upward trend. In the case of Italy, diesel vehicles are making something of a come-back. In the mid 1980s, the diesel share rose to over 25 per cent of new car sales, but fell back sharply by the beginning of the 1990s following the introduction of discriminatory vehicle taxes on diesel models. However, the fuel economy benefits of diesel vehicles are stimulating their popularity among Italian car buyers in recent years. The diesel share of new sales has more than doubled in the space of just three years, and motor industry forecasts indicate that, with the current structure of car and fuel taxation, a share of 25 per cent is achievable before the turn of the century.

Outside the four countries shown in Figure 3.1, diesel cars are not a significant part of the car stock in other western European countries in the Mediterranean. In Greece, they represent only around 2 per cent of new car sales. Diesel cars have also achieved little penetration in Switzerland. As discussed below, Switzerland is rather unusual in that diesel has traditionally been taxed (and consequently priced) at a premium to gasoline. As a result, the share of diesel-powered car sales has remained below 5 per cent during the 1990s.

Consumer attitudes towards diesel-fuelled vehicles are determined primarily by the relative capital and operational costs compared to gasoline engines. These costs are in turn heavily influenced by government, with the policy stance influenced by a weighting of efficiency and environmental concerns, for which the current conventional wisdom runs as follows. Diesel engines have a number of advantages over those designed to run on gasoline. They are, for example, considerably more efficient than their gasoline counterparts. This arises because the diesel engine has a variable stoichiometry, which means the air intake does not have to be throttled to limit it in proportion to the amount of fuel being used. Moreover, compression ratios (i.e., the extent to which the fuel/air mixture is compressed before combustion) are much higher than for gasoline engines.

Diesel engines tend to have a longer life expectancy than gasoline ones, resulting in the greater durability of diesel-powered cars. Furthermore, there is less component failure associated with the diesel engine. Because it relies on high temperature and pressure to ignite the fuel/air mixture rather than a spark, the need for some of the less reliable components of gasoline engines (such as spark plugs) is eliminated. As discussed further below, owners of diesel cars tend to enjoy lower fuel costs than drivers of gasoline-powered vehicles because, on a per gallon basis, diesel is significantly cheaper than gasoline in most countries. As far as emissions are concerned, the high fuel/air compression ratio in diesel engines results in low emissions of carbon monoxide and volatile organic compounds (VOCs). However, because the fuel burns with a very hot flame as it combines with the air, diesel engines produce moderate amounts of nitrogen oxides (NO_x). Nevertheless, as Table 3.1 shows, these emissions are still lower than those associated with a gasoline engine that has no exhaust control (although they are higher than a gasoline car fitted with a catalytic converter).

Table 3.1: Typical Emissions from Oil-Burning Technologies (grams per kilogram of fuel).

Engine Type	*CO*	*VOC*	*NO_x*	*Particulates*
Light-Duty Gasoline (No Exhaust Control)	200–300	20–30	20–40	< 0.3
Light-Duty Gasoline (With Catalytic Converter)	20–60	2–6	2–10	<0.3
Light-Duty Diesel (No Exhaust Control)	15–50	2–5	10–20	3

Source: US Environmental Protection Agency

As is seen in Table 3.1, diesel engines emit far more particulates than gasoline models. The significance of this disadvantage is growing as concerns emerge about the damage done by particulates relative to other pollutants, particularly in terms of carcinogenic properties. Other disadvantages of diesel engines include their high cost (on an equivalent power basis) compared with gasoline engines, and their lower power/weight ratios, which impair their driving performance. Because of the constant high compression ratio and high air intake associated with diesel engines, they are also noisy at low power. Moreover, in cold weather, the heavy hydrocarbons in the diesel fuel are prone to crystallisation, resulting in potential cold start problems.

In most countries, diesel is priced at a significant discount to gasoline, and the difference in tax structure is the key determination of the penetration of diesel-fuelled vehicles. While the EU has set the agenda on fuel specifications, as detailed in the next section, the EU's impact on taxation structure has to date been limited. However, with the single currency adding further impetus towards change, EU proposals provide a basis for judging in which direction the relative taxation structure is moving. To gauge this, we must establish firstly whether any narrowing of gasoil's advantage is planned, and secondly whether EU proposals are likely to be binding.

Within the EU, member states have hitherto been free to set the excise duties on motor fuels. However, in March 1997, the European Commission adopted a proposal for a Directive to widen the scope of the EU minimum tax rate system, which currently applies only to mineral oils, to all energy products. The proposal presents a consistent framework for the energy sector in the EU, whilst still allowing member states the flexibility to charge more than the minimum rates of tax. At present, only the excise duties charged on mineral oils are governed by the EU-wide system of minimum taxation, the rates of which have remained static since 1992. Because this has resulted in distortions between different sources of energy and between the member states, the Commission has proposed that all energy products be taxed, and the rates of taxation should be revised. In addition, the proposal gives member states the flexibility to differentiate the rates of taxation on the basis of environmental criteria, provided that the minimum rates are complied with.

Although environmental concerns about diesel emissions are putting pressure on governments to reduce the diesel/gasoline tax differential, there is no guarantee that this measure alone will stifle the growth in diesel use, at least in the short and medium term. This is because diesel's share of the overall fuel requirements of the road transport sector depends upon a host of other factors. For instance, as discussed above, the commercial vehicle fleet is almost entirely reliant on diesel. It is difficult to imagine a situation where gasoline is used in heavy-duty vehicles throughout Europe, unless there is a radical pricing change in favour of gasoline throughout the region. Since commercial users account for between 70 and 80 per cent of the total diesel requirements of the road transport sectors of OECD Europe, they underpin the demand for diesel in the region. Thus, diesel use can be strongly influenced by growth in commercial traffic, which, in turn, can depend on factors such as the general level of economic activity, competition for freight traffic between the different transport sectors, the use of public transport and so on.

The potential for substitution between diesel and gasoline is much greater within the non-commercial sector. Even where sales of diesel cars as a proportion of total new car sales are falling, this does not necessarily mean that the number of diesel cars in national car fleets (which will determine the level of diesel consumption) is also declining. This effect arises from the lower turnover rates of diesel-powered cars to lower turnover rates when compared with their gasoline counterparts.

3.   Environmental Specifications

One of the major capital obligations facing oil refiners is the need to comply with new strict environmental regulations, which often require large investments to modify refineries in order to meet new quality requirements. All member states of the European Union (EU), together with Norway and Switzerland, have adopted the CEN (Comité Européen de Normalisation) specifications for unleaded gasoline, diesel and automotive LPG. However, as a result of the EU's Auto-Oil Programme, the EU Commission has proposed a number of changes that will require extensive revisions of the CEN gasoline and diesel fuel specifications which, in turn, will have important implications for many refiners in the region.

Until new EU-wide legislation comes into effect at the turn of the century, most western European countries are adopting CEN specifications for unleaded gasoline and diesel fuel. In the case of leaded gasoline, countries retain their own national leaded grade specifications. The CEN specification for unleaded gasoline (EN 228:1993) has been adopted by all EU member states, together with Norway and Switzerland.

A benzene content of 5 per cent volume by weight (v/v) maximum is specified for both leaded and unleaded gasolines in the EU. Nevertheless, some countries have voluntarily adopted even lower benzene and aromatics limits. In Italy, for example, the benzene content of the total gasoline pool was limited to 3 per cent from 1 January 1993. This was on the basis of a three-month sales weighted production average for each refinery by a voluntary agreement between the Environment Ministry and the oil companies operating in the country. At the beginning of 1995, some oil companies distributed gasoline with benzene limited to a maximum of 1.8 per cent v/v. From 1 July 1997, the maximum benzene of all gasolines was reduced to 1.4 per cent v/v. This limit was then reduced further to 1.0 per cent v/v from 1 July 1999.

Meanwhile, there is a lobby, particularly within the German government, which considers that the EU Commission is not going far enough in its efforts to reduce aromatics and benzene contents in gasoline. The German Ministry of the Environment (BMU) proposes limits of 30 per cent v/v aromatics and a maximum of 1 per cent v/v benzene for all gasoline grades. Superplus gasoline with a 1 per cent v/v benzene content has been made available voluntarily by many German oil companies since October 1995.

Within the EU, the maximum lead content of leaded gasolines is required to be within the range of 0.15 to 0.40 g Pb/litre. In practice, all countries are at the lowest end of this scale. In 1985, EU Directive 85/210/EEC permitted unleaded gasoline (with a maximum of 0.013 grams of lead per litre) to be marketed. This Directive also encouraged member states to provide incentives (for example, through differential rates of taxation) to promote sales of unleaded gasoline.

For diesel, specification change has involved a forced route march from 0.5 per cent sulphur content, through 0.3 per cent and 0.2 per cent to 0.05 per cent, with the way ahead being towards 0.035 per cent and even 0.005 per cent. By 2005 the end of the march may indeed be the latter specification, which will have involved reducing sulphur content by a factor of a hundred over the course of eighteen years.

The journey began in March 1987, when the EU's Council of Environment Ministers agreed to a directive reducing the maximum sulphur content of all gasoils (except those used by shipping or for further processing) to 0.3 per cent and allowed member states to set a stricter limit of 0.2 per cent in heavily polluted areas. Member states were required to implement this directive (EEC/85/716) by 1 January 1989. This was superceded in 1993 by the more radical directive 93/12/EEC, which has two main elements. A limit of 0.2 per cent was applied for all gas oils, including diesel fuel, from 1 October 1994, and a limit of 0.05 per cent for diesel fuel to be implemented by 1 October 1996. In the interim, member states were required to ensure the 'progressive availability' of a diesel fuel with a sulphur content of 0.05 per cent 'from 1 October 1995'.

There is often a perception that Mediterranean countries have in general been laggards in implementing environmental specifications, and that Italy in particular has been a laggard in implementing any EU directive. However, in the case of directive 93/12/EEC the perception does not equate to reality. Italy conformed to the earlier EU 1994 limit of 0.2 per cent *ahead* of schedule by means of a voluntary agreement between the government and companies. Furthermore, the 0.05 per cent EU maximum was introduced in January 1995, earlier than mandated, because two Italian companies began to distribute diesel fuel of this quality in the main cities at the request of local authorities. The 0.05 per cent limit became compulsory in Italy on 1 December 1995. Some other EU member states, including Germany, voluntarily implemented the 0.05 per cent sulphur limit a year ahead of the EU Commission's October 1996 deadline. Meanwhile, in Switzerland (which tends to shadow EU specifications, but implement them quicker), the sulphur content of diesel fuel was reduced from 0.2 per cent to 0.05 per cent from 1 January 1994.

To meet the October 1996 requirement of 0.05 per cent maximum sulphur, those European refiners with modern hydro-treating capacity were able to minimise their expenditure on desulphurisation simply by modifying their existing hydrotreating units. However, for most, the stricter sulphur specifications implied the need for investment in new units. Nevertheless, all but one of the EU member states met the reduced sulphur deadline. The exception was Portugal. The 23 thousand b/d hydrotreater at Petrogal's Porto refinery and the 34 thousand barrels per day hydrotreater at Sines were not due for completion until early 1997. Thus, Portugal had to get permission from the EU to delay the introduction of 0.05 per cent sulphur diesel until these units were commissioned.

The more difficult changes came at the start of 2000 with strict new EU-wide fuel specifications. The origin of this raft of changes was the EU Auto-Oil programme, the first stage of which was completed in 1996. Auto-Oil is designed to provide European legislators with a rational scientific basis for the setting of future European vehicle exhaust emission limits for road transport on a cost-effective basis, linked to air quality needs, taking into account motor technology and fuels, as well as other technical measures such as inspection and maintenance and traffic management systems. Auto-Oil brings together the EU Commission, the European oil industry (under the auspices of EUROPIA) and the European motor industry (ACEA). This inter-industry research project, known as EPEFE (the European Programme on Emissions, Fuels and Engine Technology), was designed to advance the scientific understanding of the synergetic relationships between fuel parameters, engine technology and vehicle emissions. The results of EPEFE helped establish the relationships between fuel composition and vehicle technology and to identify and quantify what reductions in road traffic emissions could be achieved by combining advanced fuels with advanced vehicle/engine technologies. The results were embodied into tables and used to quantify complex equations that were associated with fuels and vehicle/engine technologies for inclusion into the EU Commission's Air Quality Modelling Studies. This process facilitated the search for the optimum combination of measures to achieve the EU's air quality objectives, and gave rise to the new fuel specifications.

The proposals made by the Commission in a draft Directive placed before the European Parliament and Council had three main elements. First, all gasolines had to be unleaded by 1 January 2000, unless a member state could demonstrate that this would result in severe socio-economic difficulties. In any case, all gasolines must be unleaded by 1 January 2002. Secondly, from 1 January 2000, gasolines had to comply with the specification given in Table 3.2, with limitations on gasoline volatility, aromatics and olefins. Furthermore, benzene contents were limited to 2.0 per cent v/v maximum.

The third element in the directive was the diesel specification shown in Table 3.3, which had to be met by all diesel fuels from 1 January 2000. This has higher ignition quality than the

Table 3.2: Gasoline Specification in 2000 under EU Directive.

Parameter		Limit	Test Method
RVP, kPa (Summer Period[1])	max	60	EN12
Distillation:			
evaporation @ 100°C, % v/v	min	46	ISO 3405
evaporation @ 150°C, % v/v	min	75	ISO 3405
Olefins, % v/v	max	18.0[2]	ASTM D1319
Aromatics, % v/v	max	45	ASTM D1319
Benzene, % v/v	max	2	EN 238
Oxygen Content, % m/m	max	2.3	PrEN1601
Sulphur Content, % m/m	max	0.02	ISO 8754
Lead Content, g/litre	max	0.005	EN 237

1. Summer period is defined as 1 April to 30 September
2. For unleaded regular (91RON, 81 MON), olefins limit is 21.0 max

Table 3.3: Diesel Fuel Specifications in 2000 under EU Directive.

Parameter		Limit	Test Method
Cetane Number	min	51	ISO 5165
Density @ 15°C, kg/m^3	max	845	ISO 3675
Distillation, 95 % v/v evap, °C	max	360	ISO 3405
Polycyclic Aromatic			
Hydrocarbons, % m/m	max	11	prIP 391
Sulphur Content, % m/m	max	0.04	ISO 8754

CEN specification, a limitation on polycyclic aromatic hydro-carbons and a sulphur content reduced to 0.035 per cent.

The Commission has indicated that further tightening of fuel specifications will be required by 2005 to meet anticipated anti-pollution targets. It seems likely that the stage two proposals will require further reductions in sulphur contents of fuels, with levels as low as 0.005 per cent being discussed.

The Commission has also made predictions about the impact that its proposed new fuel specifications will have on average fuel qualities in the market place and on air quality. These are shown in Table 3.4.

In specific areas where atmospheric pollution constitutes a serious and recurrent health problem, member states are

Table 3.4: Commission Prediction of Effects of Fuel Changes.

(a) Market Average Gasoline Quality in 2000

Parameter	Without Proposal	With Proposal
RVP Summer, kPa	68	58
E100, % v/v	53	53
E150, % v/v	84	84
Olefins, % v/v	11	11
Aromatics, % v/v	40	37
Benzene, % v/v	2.3	1.6
Oxygen, % m/m	0.6	1
Sulphur, ppm	300	150
Lead, g/litre	0.005	0.005

(b) Market Average Diesel Fuel Quality in 2000

Parameter	Without Proposal	With Proposal
Cetane Number	51	53
Density, g/l	843	835
Polyaromatics, % m/m	9	6
T95, °C	355	350
Sulphur, ppm	450	300

(c) Emissions Reductions from Proposed Fuel Quality Changes

Pollutant	% reduction from change in gasoline quality	% reduction from change in diesel quality
NOx	7.12	0.53
VOCs	8.44	10.68
CO	8.89	10.6
Particulates	-	9.95
Benzene	20.7	-

permitted to impose tighter fuel standards, subject to approval and conditions imposed by the Commission. It is required that member states set up a monitoring procedure to ensure compliance with the specifications, and the assistance of CEN may be sought to develop a uniform system of monitoring. From 2002, member states are required to submit to the Commission by 30 June each year a summary of the results from the national compliance monitoring programme from the previous calendar year using a common format.

For refiners, the tranche of changes that took effect in 2000 and the likely progression to far more stringent limits in 2005, are in effect a redistribution of relative advantage. Those who have already made investments are favoured, and hence there is an improvement in the comparative position of the German refineries we have classed as Mediterranean by dint of their source of crude supply. However, there will also be a redistribution of advantage among those who have already committed significant investments. In short, hydrocrackers are significantly favoured, while moving down the scale the investment demands on refiners relying heavily on thermal processes become more onerous. Refiners with catalytic crackers also face problems. While a quick fix is possible through pretreatment of cracker feed, for instance using a mild hydrocracker unit, that still leaves a cetane deficiency in the distillate, and high olefin content in gasoline. In short, except for refineries with large-scale distillate hydrocrackers, the investment costs associated with meeting the new standards on existing crude oil slates are significant.

Within the new distribution of advantage brought about by continual EU-wide tightening of specifications, the Mediterranean refiners in general have been disadvantaged. The process is one of tightening rules for northern Europe, and Mediterranean refiners need to make further investments to catch up. These investments are essentially continue or exit decisions, with little or no rate of return accruing to the capital spent. Given this, Portugal, Italy, Spain and Greece all asked for extensions in complying with the limits imposed in 2000.[1] Partial exemptions were allowed by the EU Environment Directorate, just twelve days before the 1 January 2000 deadline. All three countries were given a further two years grace in phasing out leaded gasoline, with Portugal also receiving an extra year for meeting sulphur limits in diesel, and two years for meeting sulphur limits in gasoline.

4.   Heavy Fuel Oil Demand

As was shown in the overall Mediterranean balance in Table 1.2, the region has a deficit of fuel oil, which represented 1.9 million b/d out of the 9.0 mb/d total demand in 1998. There are two facets of the potential evolution of the market, a quantity surplus appearing as the deficit rapidly disappears, and a quality imbalance between high and low sulphur fuel oil. The major cause for this is very specific, namely the policy of the Italian electricity generator ENEL (Ente Nazionale per l'Energia Elettrica), which dominates the demand side of the Mediterranean fuel oil market, and ENEL's movement to not only lower quantities of fuel oil but also to a tighter sulphur specification. Further out, changes in EU policy may exacerbate the trend, in particular the increasing attention being given to the sulphur content of bunker fuel. The bunker market, with its acceptance of fuel oil of up to 4 per cent sulphur content, represents a major 'quality dump'. Should that dump become less accommodating, the situation of excess high sulphur and tight low sulphur fuel oil supplies would become even more problematic.

The generation of electricity represents one of the fastest growing sources of demand for energy and is the largest single energy market in many Mediterranean countries. Even in the OECD countries, with almost universal electrification, electricity consumption continues to grow on average at 1 to 2 per cent or more per annum. In the non-OECD countries as a whole, where electricity demand in many countries is still widely unsatisfied, its use grows faster than GDP, and consumption has increased at an average of over 7 per cent per annum in recent years. This above average growth stems from a mixture of the modernisation of industrial and agricultural production, the growth of tourism and the spread of electricity connections to households and services, all allied to greater prosperity. The potential for a sustained and high level of growth in electricity use remains considerable.

Table 3.5 shows the mix of fuels used in power generation across selected countries. The input slate varies greatly, largely depending on the availability of indigenous energy or whether government policy is strongly focused on one energy source. The latter is the case in France where over 85 per cent of electricity is generated by nuclear power. The availability of surplus nuclear capacity in this country means that even the intermediate generating load is based on nuclear so that it is generally only the peak load that is left to other sources. The

Table 3.5:   Fuel Use in Power Generation. Selected Countries. 1996.
Million Tonnes of Oil Equivalent.

	Oil	Coal	Gas	Nuclear	Hydro and Renewables	Total
OECD						
France (all)	1.3	7.3	0.6	103.6	5.8	118.5
Greece	1.9	6.9	-	-	0.4	9.2
Hungary	1.0	2.4	1.3	3.7	<0.1	8.4
Italy	22.7	5.4	6.5	-	5.9	40.5
Portugal	0.8	2.7	-	-	1.3	4.8
Spain (all)	2.0	12.6	0.2	14.7	3.5	32.9
Turkey	1.1	8.1	3.3	-	3.6	16.0
Non-OECD						
Algeria	0.2	-	5.6	-	<0.1	5.8
Croatia	0.3	<0.1	0.2	-	0.6	1.1
Cyprus	0.7	-	-	-	-	0.7
Egypt	4.7	-	6.9	-	0.9	12.6
Israel	2.2	4.9	<0.1	-	<0.1	7.1
Libya	3.6	-	-	-	-	3.6
Malta	0.6	-	-	-	-	0.6
Morocco	1.3	1.3	-	-	0.2	2.8
Serbia	0.2	7.2	<0.1	-	1.0	8.0
Syria	2.5	-	1.2	-	0.6	4.4
Tunisia	0.3	-	1.5	-	<0.1	1.8

Sources: Own calculations from International Energy Agency, *Energy Balances of OECD Countries*, 1999 edition and *Energy Statistics of non-OCED Countries*, 1998 edition.

use of diesel generators is low and only negligible amounts of electricity are generated from fuel oil-fired power plants.

Coal-fired power stations are the largest hydrocarbon source of electricity in Turkey, Greece and Spain. All are based almost entirely on indigenous hard coal or lignite. However, any new power stations that are planned are based mainly on natural gas-fuelled turbines. In Spain, despite increased output from nuclear power stations and some increase in local coal use, fuel oil use has also increased slightly in recent years. However, much depends on the level of rainfall as the fuel oil plants tend to be used to make up for shortfalls of power from hydro plants at times of drought. None the less, even in a poor year for rainfall, fuel oil generates less than 10 per cent of electricity in

Spain. The use of diesel generators within the universal and established systems of most of the OECD countries is confined largely to standby equipment or peak shaving.

In most of the non-OECD Mediterranean countries, except Libya and Israel, there is a substantial shortfall between the availability of electricity from utility networks and its demand. This stems from an inadequate level of investment to meet the very substantial amounts of new generating capacity and new grid systems required. Diesel and other light fuel oils are still widely used for electricity generation in small non-connected power plants, partly because of shortcomings in the utility supply.

The high growth rate of the demand for electricity continues to be met by new oil-fired power plants in a few countries, most notably Libya, where oil remains the main source of power. In Egypt, which is by far the largest user of electricity in this group of countries, oil use is stagnating in the face of the construction of new gas turbines based on indigenous gas. Algeria and Tunisia already generate over 90 per cent of their electricity from natural gas and Syria is moving in the same direction. Where gas is available then oil's share in electricity generation has fallen. Israel and Morocco, without any significant natural gas of their own, have based much of their recent expansion in capacity on coal-fired plant which has resulted in only very minor increases in oil use.

The key feature of Table 3.5 is the extent to which Italy dominates the market. Italy consumes over three-quarters of the fuel oil used in power generation in the OECD part of the Mediterranean, and a half of consumption in the region as a whole. Within the Italian total, all bar 3 million tonnes was bought by ENEL, which generates the bulk of Italian electricity, 173.1 TWh in 1996 compared to 42.9 TWh by private companies and 9.2 TWh by other public utilities. This makes ENEL the third largest generator in the world, only eclipsed by EdF (Electricité de France) and by TEPCO (Tokyo Electric Power Company).

ENEL's demand for fuel oil has been falling at about 4.5 per cent per annum since 1995, and we would expect this decline to accelerate sharply before 2005, due to a combination of factors. The major one is a greater attention to cost and efficiency on the part of ENEL itself, which is faced with two main imperatives. First is imminent privatisation. Prior to this ENEL has been restructured into a holding company with separate generation, transmission and distribution arms. The associated introduction of transfer pricing and the transformation of cross subsidies from opaqueness into highly transparent accounting items, has produced a more aggressive stance towards costs, as opposed to the, to say the least, more relaxed attitude that ENEL had before restructuring.

The second imperative ENEL faces is the opening up of the Italian electricity sector, primarily driven by the EU directive 96/92 of 19 December 1996. Under this directive ENEL cannot have any exclusive rights over production, imports or infrastructure, and would have to relinquish 30 per cent of the market. While implementation is late, the directive will eventually be met (ENEL's own conservative estimate is 2003[2]), and it is already shaping the investment decisions of both ENEL and its potential and actual competitors. In all cases, those decisions imply the mothballing of significant amounts of oil-fired capacity, and the construction of combined-cycle gas plants.

To add to the strain on the heavy fuel oil market, officially Italy is moving from the current 1 per cent sulphur limit in fuel oil towards a universal 0.25 per cent limit. On the one hand, Italy's record at implementing specification changes is very good, as was noted in the last section. On the other, fast implementation of the standard means running into problems in sourcing enough local material, and thus may be constrained by the pace of refinery upgrading. However, in terms of refinery configurations for the future, it is clear that any Italian refiner intending to supply fuel oil into the local power market will have to meet the lower sulphur specification.

5.   Incremental Mediterranean Oil Demand

The first key point to be made about Mediterranean energy demand is that we are dealing with a large but disparate region, made up of an area of high income combined with static population, and one of low income but fast population growth. Under the expanded definition of the Mediterranean used in the previous chapter, the area encompasses a population of some 400 million people. In OECD areas of the Mediterranean (with the exception of Turkey), population growth is slow, with a total of some 1.5 million increase each year. Elsewhere in the region, population growth is fast and provides a major source of underlying energy demand growth. The combined population growth in Turkey, Algeria, Morocco and Egypt alone amounts to some 4 million each year.

In terms of national income, the differences are just as marked, with GDP per head at over $20,000 (measured in real 1990 US dollars) in Italy, France and Germany compared, for example, with well under $1000 in Egypt. This contrast between the mainly highly developed and very prosperous countries of the north with their ageing and stagnating populations and the relatively undeveloped countries of the south and east with their young and fast growing populations has some significance in terms of economics and politics. The population growth in the south also has a remorseless impact, with each generation having higher aspirational levels, on energy demand.

The amount of energy consumed also varies widely between countries, largely reflecting the difference in stages of their economic development. Around 2 to 3 tonnes of oil equivalent (toe) are currently consumed per person in the Mediterranean OECD countries other than Turkey. Elsewhere, consumption is generally at around 1 toe per capita or below. Israel, with its advanced industrial and military complexes, and Libya, with the energy consumption of the oil sector, are exceptions with

Table 3.6: Shares of Oil and Natural Gas in Primary Energy Demand. Selected Countries. 1996. Per Cent.

	Oil	*Gas*	*Oil and Gas*
France (all)	37.4	11.9	49.3
Turkey	47.9	12.5	60.4
Greece	63.6	<1	63.6
Spain (all)	58.3	8.3	66.6
Israel	72.7	<1	72.7
Morocco	76.1	<1	76.1
Tunisia	611	27.0	88.1
Italy	60.0	29.9	89.9
Egypt	66.5	27.8	92.3
Libya	74.1	25.3	99.4
Algeria	29.6	69.5	99.1

levels of energy consumption similar to the OECD of around 3 toe per capita. Although economic differences are largely behind these significant differences in consumption, climate and the mixture of fuels and pattern of activity also play significant roles.

Oil and gas are the dominant primary fuels in the south as they are in most of the OECD countries, as is shown in Table 3.6, with countries listed in ascending order of their percentage use of oil and gas. The proportion of oil used, at around 30 per cent of primary energy consumption, is at its lowest in Algeria, with its extensive and highly utilised gas resources. Elsewhere, oil's contribution is generally well over 50 per cent. Other than in France, with its heavy politically inspired reliance on nuclear electricity, oil and gas provide over 50 per cent of the energy needs of all the major countries in the Mediterranean.

Electricity consumption, usually a good indicator of development, is well above 3000 kwh per capita in all the OECD countries except Turkey. In France and Germany it is over 6000 kwh per capita and there is some surplus generating capacity. In the south, the new generating capacity needed to meet the present unsatisfied demand is very substantial. With the exceptions of Libya, Israel and Cyprus, consumption has yet to reach much more than 1000 kwh per capita. In Turkey, for example, it is only just over 1000 kwh and in Morocco it is as low as 450 kwh per capita.

As is shown in Table 3.7, with countries listed in descending order of percentage oil demand increase over the 1990s, the growth in demand has been relatively strong in the majority of countries over the decade. There are three main groupings of countries. The first, consisting of France, Italy, Switzerland, Austria and southern Germany, has shown very low rates of oil demand in the 1990s. Any positive effects arising from the price falls of 1986, and any associated boosting of demand, had played out by 1990, and since then low rates of economic growth have combined with improvements in energy efficiency and further substitution away from oil to leave the level of oil demand static.

The second group comprises the other OECD Mediterranean countries, in particular Spain, Greece and Turkey. In absolute terms, it has been these countries that have kept Mediterranean demand relatively buoyant over the last decade. Between 1985 and 1996, the three countries combined added 34 million tonnes

Table 3.7:   Oil Consumption and Demand Growth. Selected Countries. 1985, 1990 and 1996. Million Tonnes and Per Cent per Annum.

	1985	1990	1996	Annual % Growth 1990–96
Lebanon	2.2	2.1	4.9	15.2
Libya	7.0	7.4	12.0	8.5
Tunisia	2.6	2.3	3.3	6.2
Israel	6.1	9.2	12.5	5.3
Turkey	16.8	22.1	28.8	4.6
Cyprus	1.0	1.5	1.9	4.1
Syria	7.9	9.4	11.9	4.0
Morocco	4.3	5.1	6.3	3.6
Spain (all)	42.9	48.7	58.7	3.2
Greece	12.0	15.7	18.5	2.8
Algeria	8.0	8.3	9.4	2.2
Croatia	3.0	3.8	4.1	1.3
Germany (all)	126.3	127.3	137.4	1.3
Austria	9.8	10.8	11.4	0.9
Egypt	20.8	23.8	24.6	0.6
France (all)	84.3	89.4	91.0	0.3
Italy	84.4	93.6	94.1	0.1
Switzerland	12.0	12.8	12.2	-0.8
Bosnia	0.9	1.2	1.0	-3.0

to oil demand (i.e. some 700 thousand barrels per day). Strong economic growth has been combined with a high income elasticity of demand for oil products, and particularly strong growth in transportation demand. The third group consists of non-OECD countries, primarily with high rates of demand growth. However, within this group gas substitution for oil is dampening growth in Egypt, the largest consumer.

To provide indications of the ranges in the scale of incremental future demand, while various country specific factors have been used, the broad assumptions we have used in projecting demand differ by the groups defined above. In the first group, consisting of those countries with the highest per capita incomes, we have assumed that energy use in general maintains the relatively high income elasticity experienced in the 1990s. All of the easy energy efficiency options have been taken, and in particular household use of energy is increasing fast. For instance, the average living space per person is increasing with the reduction in average household size. With the real price of energy falling for domestic non-transportation uses, operating costs are becoming less significant than capital costs, and incomes are surging ahead of both. Hence, households have more appliances, and on average, those appliances are consuming more energy. In total, the above implies high rates of growth for electricity demand, but only has a bearing on oil demand in a few areas. In particular, the only product likely to gain significantly is gasoline, with demand being pushed by more cars on the road, and those cars becoming bigger and less fuel efficient, for instance the sharp expansion in the use of four-wheeled drive cars. In total, oil demand will grow in these countries (with the exception of Italy), but at relatively modest rates.

For the second group, comprising the rest of the OECD countries within the Mediterranean, we have assumed relatively high rates of GDP growth. For non-OECD countries, we have assumed in general continuing economic growth, but no normalisation in those countries where economic growth is held back by politics. For the countries of central Europe and the Balkans, we have assumed no dramatic economic take-off.

Projections are rather dry statistics whose usefulness erodes very quickly. Rather than present a full set of projections, here we solely seek to take stock of the likely scale of increments. Overall, our calculations suggest that Mediterranean demand is increasing at a rate of some 1.2 and 1.5 million b/d over a ten-year period, with Spain, Turkey and Greece accounting for about half the increment. The main point of this exercise is that the potential absorption capacity of Mediterranean demand is limited. That scale of absolute demand increase over a decade is small relative to potential swings in supply, particularly from proximate producers to the Mediterranean such as Iraq, Russia and the Caspian. The potential swings in export capacity in these countries are large enough to swamp the gradual increases in Mediterranean demand and would thus transmit through to changes in the world oil market as a whole. In the Asian and US markets it is fluctuation of demand that is the main mover of the market. In the Mediterranean that role is taken by supply.

Notes

1. France was the only other country to ask for an extension, but only for sales in its overseas territories.
2. Franco Tatò (ENEL Chief Executive) quoted in *Electricity International*, March 1998.

4 THE MEDITERRANEAN PRODUCERS

1. Introduction

Petroleum reserves are distributed very widely across Mediterranean countries, but they are also distributed extremely unevenly. Of the countries we have defined as Mediterranean on the basis of the sourcing of crude oil input to refineries, no less than twenty have some indigenous oil resources. However, as is shown in Table 4.1, only five have proved reserves greater than 500 million barrels, and the same five are the only countries with production levels greater than 100 thousand barrels per day. The other fifteen countries share just 3.5 per cent of regional reserves and 9 per cent of production.

Table 4.1: Reserves and Production. Selected Countries. End of 1999 and 1999 average. Million Barrels and Thousand Barrels per Day.

	Reserves mb	Production th b/d
Libya	29500	1336
Egypt	2948	851
Algeria	9200	766
Syria	2500	537
Italy	622	101
Tunisia	308	83
Turkey	299	68
Germany	357	55
France	107	31
Croatia	92	25
Hungary	110	24
Austria	86	21
Serbia	78	18
Spain	14	6
Albania	165	6
Czech Republic	15	7
Slovakia	9	2
Israel	4	<1
Morocco	2	<1
Greece	10	0

Source: *Oil and Gas Journal*, 20 December 1999

In the context of the world market, production within the Mediterranean is relatively insignificant. The production level of Libya, as shown in Table 4.1, gives it the ranking of the world's fifteenth largest producer, while Egypt ranks as twentieth. For the Mediterranean as a whole, oil reserves are just 4 per cent of the world total and production levels 6 per cent. With two-thirds of those reserves and one-third of production occurring in Libya, the global significance of the other Mediterranean producers is trifling. Their importance is then primarily at the margin within the regional context. The fifteen countries in the tail of Table 4.1 are not very prospective areas, and while exploration continues in Greece and Turkey in particular, the path of regional output will be primarily determined by what happens in the five main producing countries.

2. Libya

The prospect of revival in Libyan exploration and development, and ultimately in output, has been enhanced by the lifting of UN sanctions but remains muted due to the continuation of the US unilateral sanctions regime. After a dearth of exploration activity in the 1980s, upstream activity increased in the early 1990s before being depressed by UN sanctions. Although the sanctions imposed under UN Resolution 883 in 1993 as part of a general tightening of measures against the country complicated the process of oil industry development, they are not the only, or indeed the major, reason for the decline in the fortunes of the Libyan oil industry. Many of Libya's fields have been in operation for more than thirty years, and depletion is well entrenched. Indeed, enhanced recovery technology was needed well before the strengthening of UN sanctions. Moreover, European countries whose companies are involved in the Libyan oil sector managed to obstruct UN restrictions on the trade of oilfield equipment with Libya, and restrictions on oilfield equipment itself were not overtly imposed.

However, while they lasted UN sanctions did have some impact on activity, although the strength of that effect depends on which indicator is chosen. Table 4.2 shows some possible indicators, demonstrating that the impact depended on stages

Table 4.2: Libyan Oil Exploration Activity, 1987–98.

	87	88	89	90	91	92	93	94	95	96	97	98
Seismic Activity (crew/months)	96	127	115	143	165	117	106	64	58	81	42	73
Drilling Rigs (no. at year end)	15	20	17	15	15	30	28	25	13	21	19	19
E & D Wells Drilled	41	100	87	98	94	94	106	100	88	131	128	116
Distance Drilled (km)	123	271	258	255	269	275	253	301	265	291	276	255
No. of Oil Discoveries	0	4	4	5	3	1	8	5	4	3	2	6

Source: *OAPEC Annual Reports*, various issues

of development. The more that capital was locked, the less effect there was, while at the earlier relatively lower cost stages, activity was curtailed. In the latter category, seismic activity fell away sharply after 1993. In the former, the number of wells drilled increased after 1993, and the series for the distance drilled also shows no signs of discontinuity.

Despite the robustness of some of the indicators shown in Table 4.2, the scale of activity in Libya is not commensurate with the country's prospectivity or importance within the reserve base of the region. For example, Libya has about eight times the reserves of Egypt, and three times those of Algeria. It would also generally be considered far more prospective than Egypt, and at least as prospective as Algeria. However, in 1998 262 kilometres were drilled in Algeria, and 480 kilometres in Egypt, compared to Libya's 255 kilometres. The potential scope of any upturn in activity remains considerable.

On the positive side for Libya, projects launched before the imposition of the United States Iran Libya Sanctions Act (ILSA) in August 1996 have begun to produce larger than expected incremental supplies. Beyond US legislation, while the multilateral sanctions imposed by the United Nations lasted, they had dampened the enthusiasm of foreign investors and deprived Libya of the technology required for enhanced oil recovery which would boost production from ageing structures. As a result, Libya's major established oilfields have experienced rapidly declining output over the last five years. Whilst new flows have come on stream, reserve replacement through the 1980s and 1990s has not been sufficient to offset the slide. Ultimately, it is likely that the continuation of US sanctions will not prevent the development of the Libyan oil industry. With the cost of production for Libyan oil among the lowest in the world, sometimes as low as $0.65/barrel, Libya remains of interest to exploration companies.

Despite some significant new discoveries, it is difficult to envisage significant growth in total Libyan production until the increasingly rapid decline in some of the major producing fields is stemmed. Figure 4.1 shows the resultant stagnation in Libyan crude oil production. The state owned National Oil Company (NOC) had planned to launch a programme to increase capacity to 2 million b/d, through the expansion of facilities at existing fields and the development of new streams. However, the imposition of sanctions in 1992, their tightening in 1993, and Libya's general lack of funds meant that the programme was stalled.

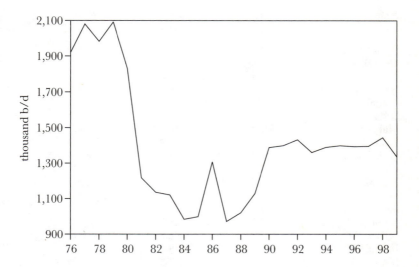

Figure 4.1: Libyan Crude Oil Production. 1976–99. Thousand Barrels per Day

Source: OPEC *Annual Statistical Bulletin*, various years, and *Oil and Gas Journal*

NOC, through its interests in numerous operating companies, controls about 80 per cent of Libyan production. Agoco is the biggest such venture, with current output of 450 thousand b/d, followed by the Waha Oil Company, producing 400 thousand b/d, and the Sirte Oil Company, with 85 thousand b/d. Of the foreign operators, ENI is by far the most important and long-standing (since 1966) producer in Libya, with a current output of over 200 thousand b/d. The main Libyan fields are shown in Table 4.3 and the output totals for the key producers are shown in Table 4.4.

The current position of the fields run by affiliates of NOC is weak, with sanctions having taken a heavy toll of initiatives to hold production at steady levels, and to boost output from new streams. In fact, output is now falling at a rate of 8 per cent per annum. Sirte and Waha have both failed to return production to anything like their levels before the imposition of sanctions.

Table 4.3:   Recoverable Reserves of Major Libyan Oil Fields. Million Barrels.

Field	Gravity °API	Date of Discovery	Reserves (mb)
Baha	43.4	1958	600
Dahra/Hofra	37–41	1958	700
Amal	37.5	1959	4,250
Nasser (Zelten)	38	1959	2,200
Waha	36	1959	1,200
Beda	36	1959	900
Mabruk	35–38	1959	385
Defa	35.6	1960	1,800
Sarir "C"	37.2	1961	3,650
Gialo	35.7	1961	4,000
Raguba	n.a.	1961	1,000
Samah	33.4	1961	500
Sarir "L"	36.8	1964	1,080
Nafoora/Augila	35.5	1965	1,500
Intisar "D"	39	1967	1,200
Intisar "A"	45	1967	750
Bu Attifel	41	1968	1,000
Mesla	36	1971	1,500
Bouri	26	1977	670
Murzuk	43	1984	750
Elephant	39	1997	1,000 (in place)

Table 4.4: Libyan Crude Oil Production by Operator. February 1998.
Thousand Barrels per Day.

Operator	Field	Production
Agoco	Sarir North/Sarir	200
	Nafoora/Augila	120
	Mesla	130
ENI	Bu Attifel	110
	Rimal-Khatib	10
	Bouri	110
OMV	Intisar	65
Repsol	Murzuk	75
Veba	Amal	50
	Hofra	5
	Ora	5
	Ghani/Zeinat/Zala	20
Total	Mabruk	12
Sirte	Nasser (Zelten)	60
	Raguba/Others	25
Waha	Waha	400
Wintershall	al-Sarah	50
	al-Nakhla	15
Total Libya		1462

Source: *PIW*, 2 March 1998

The slump in production from Libya's oldest fields – Brega, Sarir, Sirtica, Waha and Zueitina – has been of the order of 250 thousand b/d since 1992, when the first wave of sanctions was imposed.

In the aftermath of the nationalisation of the Libyan oil industry in 1973, numerous production-sharing agreements were signed with foreign oil companies. As US companies began to leave in 1982 after the US trade embargo was announced, about thirty, mostly European companies stayed on, some of whom now have exploration/production agreements with NOC. Foremost among these is ENI, which in 1993 signed a major agreement with NOC, broadening the scope of previous development arrangements, and giving the Italians improved financial terms for existing agreements, as well as the right to acquire five new blocks.

In addition to the application of enhanced oil recovery (EOR) to older fields, Libya's plans to increase output focus on three key fields. The Bouri field, discovered in 1976, is the largest producing field in the Mediterranean basin, with 4 to 5 billion barrels of 24° API gravity crude in place, of which 650 million barrels are recoverable. The first development phase was completed by ENI, the operator, in 1990. The second field is Murzuk, with proven recoverable reserves of about 750 million barrels of 43° API gravity. Repsol leads a consortium also comprising OMV and Total. Current output is 75 thousand b/d, but is due to reach 100 thousand b/d by the end of 1998. This will depend upon completion of a second pipeline system north to Zaita on the coast, where Murzuk crude is currently refined.

The pace of discoveries has slowed in recent years, although during the 1990s a few continued to be made each year. The most important of these is the giant Elephant field, found by LASMO, in January 1998 in the Murzuk basin. At an estimated 1 billion barrels in place, this is probably the most important find in Libya since Murzuk in 1984, and is being developed by LASMO in conjunction with ENI and a Korean consortium.

In early 1988, the Libyan government announced new, improved exploration and production-sharing agreements for onshore and offshore acreage to foreign oil companies. The new round, EPSA III, was designed to be more attractive than previous PSAs, and indeed succeeded in attracting numerous companies, such that by the end of 1995, there were 25 foreign interests exploring for oil in Libya. Although only a handful of upstream deals have been signed between Libya and foreign companies since the passage of the US ILSA, a number of European and other companies have remained keen to acquire acreage. Details of the agreements signed for exploration activities since 1989 are provided in Table 4.5 below.

Given the current political climate, the Libyan oil industry is likely to be constrained for a while. Developmental growth will continue to be hampered principally by international political obstacles, with consequential financial and technical difficulties impacting on the sector. The current rate of decline of the more mature Libyan oilfields is the most serious threat to long-term output growth.

The lifting of sanctions on Libya is happening as a two-stage

Table 4.5: Libyan Exploration Agreements Signed Under EPSA III. 1989–98.

Company	Date	Block	Area (sq. km)
INA-Naftaplin	Jul-89	SS, OO, HH, KK, FI (Sirte Basin)	257, 265, 299, 211, 247
OMV, Braspetrol, Husky Oil	Aug-89	NC 162 (Ghadames)	6560
Braspetrol, OMV, Husky Oil	Aug-89	NC 166 (Sirte Basin)	10,590
OMV, Husky	Aug-89	NC 163, 164 and 165 (Sirte Basin)	3,507
INA-Naftaplin	Dec-89	OB (off Zuwara)	2250
Petrofina, Chieftain, Scirocco Energy, PanCanadian, Yukong, Hyundai, Lucky Goldstar	Feb-90	NC 170, NC 171, NC 172 (Sirte Basin)	7,081. 6,876, 1,779
LASMO, Pedco, Hyundai, Daewoo, Majuko, Daesung	Oct-90	NC 173 (Gulf of Sirte), NC 174 (Murzuk Basin)	23,632, 11,310
IPC, Hardy Oil, Sands Petroleum	May-92	NC 176 (Sirte Basin)	n.a.
IPC	May-92	NC 177 (Sirte Basin), C 178 (Cyrenaica)	21,884
Agip	Dec-93	Four blocks (Ghadames), One block (Sirte Basin), (EPSA III Amendment of 1974 PSA)	n.a.
PanCanadian, Clyde, Yukong, Gulf Canada	Jun-96	Two blocks (North Sirte Basin)	5,000
Elf, Wintershall	Apr-97	137N and 137S (Libyan/Tunisian Waters), (EPSA III Amendment of 1974 PSA)	n.a.
Nimir, Petronas	May-97	7th November (Libyan/Tunisian Waters)	3000
Can Oxy, Bula	Oct-97	U - Ghadames Basin, G - Sirte Basin	n.a.
Repsol,Total, OMV	Nov-97	A and B (Murzuk Basin)	23000
IPC, LASMO, Hardy Oil	Apr-89	NC 154, NC 155, NC 156 (Sirte Basin)	588, 226, 118

process, the realised lifting on UN sanctions and the future lifting of US sanctions. The position of the USA remains a significant obstacle, and a constraint not only on US companies but also on some major non-US companies. In that sense, Libya's ability to realise its full potential in oil production will remain constrained until the US position becomes more amenable. After that point one should not underestimate that potential, the region is highly prospective and attractive to foreign capital. However, one should also not underestimate the time lags involved in unwinding what has been a long period of under-investment.

3.   Algeria

Libya has had political stability, but faced sanctions. Algeria has faced no sanctions, but has had no political stability. There has never been a particularly close relationship between internal domestic politics and the ease of access to oil reserves by foreign capital. What relationship exists is often an inverse one, as internal stability and economics deteriorate, governments become more receptive to foreign capital, partly to compensate for a lack of domestic capital resources, and partly to increase the interest of foreign governments in shoring up the regime. Algeria represents a case in point, where the vicious downwards spiral of political, economic and human circumstances has coincided with sea changes in the organisation of the oil sector. However, it would be wrong to suggest that the political situation in Algeria has not affected the pace of oil industry development. It clearly has increased the costs of operating in the country, and introduced a strong element of political risk assessment into development. Despite that, the oil industry can deal with political instability in Algeria, but the political obstructionism of the USA represents a more insuperable barrier.

While the counterfactual case is of course unobservable, the political situation does appear to have impacted severely on the scale of development in Algeria. To take but one metric for this, in each of the years from 1995 to 1998, the total foreign exploration budget in Algeria was at its lowest levels since 1986. In the case of several companies it does also appear to have affected the timing of investment, particularly in the immediate years after the imposition of the state of emergency in 1992. However, despite the political collapse, development has proceeded and the signing of contracts continued after the declaration of the emergency. While politics have been tumultuous, the opening up of Algeria to foreign capital was not the result of political or military collapse, but instead came from the interrelated economic, demographic and social pressures, and in particular the weakening caused by the downwards pressure on oil prices in the 1980s, culminating in the 1986 price collapse and the rapid expansion to a crippling level of Algeria's external debt.

In the 1980s, the Algerian upstream was suffering from a lack of investment, and increasingly the weakening economy was reducing the capital base from which to finance any large-scale acceleration of oil development. This lack of investment, combined with less than rigorous field maintenance, caused a ratchet effect. Algeria shared in the general OPEC reduction in exports caused by the price defence policy of the early 1980s, but post 1986 when demand began to pick up again, it was in no position to take a share of that incremental demand. As is shown in Figure 4.2, after peaking close to 1.2 million b/d, Algerian production declined steadily throughout the early 1980s. After 1986, when production started to head back towards full capacity, the second peak in 1990 was at the production level of only 0.8 million b/d. Over the course of the 1980s, one-third of Algerian production capacity had been lost.

Without some form of drastic intervention being made, the sector appeared to be hard pushed to simply maintain its existing production levels. Given the long lags involved, the sense of pessimism on the prospects for exports was maintained well into the 1990s. The production profile remains unbalanced, with the giant Hassi-Messaoud field providing the bulk of total production and dominating the production profile.

Capital scarcity within the oil sector provided the impetus for the creation of incentives for foreign capital to enter Algeria, as did the consideration of the impact of immediate signing on bonuses with the context of the overall fiscal situation. The seminal change in policy came with the enactment of the 1986 Hydrocarbon Law, allowing exploration and production (the latter in association with Sonatrach, the state oil company) by

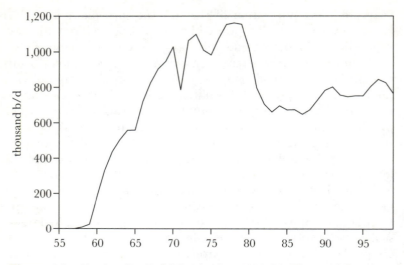

Figure 4.2:   Algerian Crude Oil Production. 1955–99. Thousand Barrels
per Day

Source: OPEC *Annual Statistical Bulletin*, various years, and *Oil and Gas Journal*

foreign capital, and the opening up of acreage. Significant
changes to this 1986 law, and a relaxation of terms, came in
amendments promulgated in December 1991. The original law
had ruled out any associations in fields discovered before 1986,
the amendments (or to be exact in this case a deletion from the
original law) opened up the possibility of joint ventures in the
existing fields.

Fiscal conditions were also changed by the 1991 revisions. In
the 1986 Hydrocarbon Law, royalty rates and taxation were
made functions of exploration and production conditions. The
normal rates were 20 per cent royalty and 85 per cent tax, with
downwards revision possible for the more difficult acreage to a
minimum of 12.5 per cent royalty and 65 per cent tax. The
fiscal system is zonal with three main categories of acreage.
Zone O (20 per cent royalty, 85 per cent tax) is in the immediate
vicinity of existing fields. Zone A (16.25 per cent royalty and 75
per cent tax) and Zone B (12.5 per cent royalty and 65 per cent
tax) are less accessible and complex in terms of exploration and
development. The 1991 revisions kept this structure in place,

but increased the extent to which more generous terms could be offered, down to 10 per cent royalty and 42 per cent tax. These changes combined with the Complementary Financial Law of September 1991, which allowed the avoidance of double taxation. It is worth noting that before this latter change, no North American or British company had signed a contract in Algeria (with the exception of Anadarko which is arguably a special case given Sonatrach's 12 per cent shareholding in the company). The attractiveness to inflowing capital was further enhanced by allowing the direct recourse to international law and arbitration.

Contracts have been awarded as production-sharing agreements, joint ventures and exploration contracts. The major conditions attached beyond fiscal and royalty issues, include the number of wells to be drilled and the length of seismic to be shot and interpreted. Among the agreements signed, the major discoveries, and the major future production increments, have come in the Ghadames basin close to the borders with Tunisia and Libya. In particular, prolific discoveries have been made in the Hassi Berkine area (block 404) and in adjoining areas. Figure 4.3 shows the exploration blocks in the area, together with the oil and condensate fields discovered to date, the company interests and the dates of the relevant production agreements. The shares shown by company are those currently operative after farm ins at the exploration stage (i.e. before the Sonatrach share is activated at any production stage).

As of 1999, production has commenced from three of the areas shown in Figure 4.3. The earliest exploration successes were made by ENI in block 403a, and its Bir Rebaa North field began production in June 1995. With the addition of Bir Rebaa West and Bir Rebaa South West streams, output now stands at about 70 thousand b/d. In Block 406a, the CEPSA discovery Rhourde El Khrouf, (RKF), a field of some 150 million barrels of reserves, began producing in June 1996 at 8 thousand b/d, before production was ramped up to 20 thousand b/d in July 1997. At the production stage Sonatrach has a 60 per cent interest for the twelve-year life of the joint venture. Like the BRN fields, RKF oil follows a spur pipeline north to intercept the main pipeline from El Borma to Hassi Messaoud.

The third producing field is Hassi Berkine South (HBNS)

which lies solely in block 404, and is again light (42° API), extremely sweet, and relatively cheap to develop and produce.[1] The development of Hassi Berkine involves the construction of what is in effect a regional processing and transportation hub. The full production plan involves the completion of three production trains of 60 thousand b/d capacity, with production having started on completion of the first train in May 1998. When the second stage is completed and all three trains are in operation, capacity will therefore have reached 180 thousand b/d. The transportation infrastructure for Hassi Berkine South and adjoining fields comes in the form of the Nezla pipeline,[2] which will take the oil on to the Hassi Messaoud facilities.

Two of the largest fields in Figure 4.3 are yet to be exploited. Both lie, at least partially, in block 404. Of these the jewel is the Qoubba field, straddling blocks 404, 405 and 406a, which to date is by some distance the most significant find achieved by outside capital. Indeed, in terms of Algeria's overall reserves, it would appear to be second only to the Hassi Messaoud field itself. A unitisation agreement between the parties involved in the three blocks, prior to establishing shares and developing a full production plan, was signed in early 1997, with Sonatrach becoming the operator of the unitised field. Qoubba appears to be a large field (estimates suggest 1 to 2 billion barrels of gross reserves and a recovery factor approaching 50 per cent), with oil from the primary pay zone being light (about 40° API) and virtually sulphur free. Simply using the usual rough rules of thumb on the basis of Qoubba's recoverable reserve base would suggest that sustainable peak production rates are potentially of the order of some 200 to 300 thousand barrels per day.

While Qoubba is not yet fully delineated or appraised, the other two major fields in block 404 are closer to a production start. The Hassi Berkine field (HBN), found by the Anadarko consortium, and the Hassi Berkine North field (HBNN), found by ENI, are the same structure. Unitisation of the HBN/HBNN field involves planned production of about 70 thousand b/d starting in 1999. Logically, it could be assumed that this development would involve the construction of a fourth processing chain at the Hassi Berkine South facility, and hence evacuation of HBN/HBNN oil along the Nezla pipeline.

Were the fields shown in Figure 4.3 the only source of

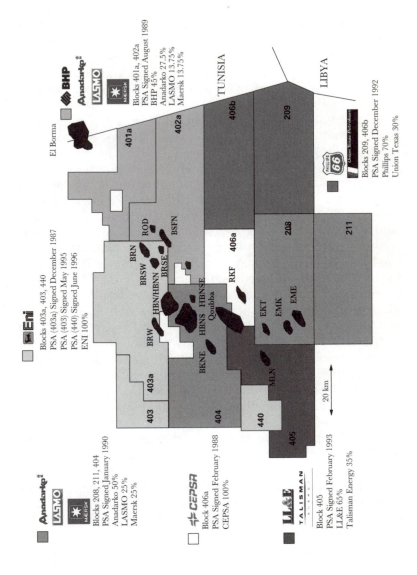

Figure 4.3: Hassi Berkine Area Exploration Blocks

incremental Algerian production, the overall rise would still be notable. However, there are a series of further developments in progress or already in operation which also constitute a significant source of increase. The most important of these are the Rhourde El Baguel EOR project, and a series of smaller new fields detailed below.

As noted above, the amendments made in 1991 to the 1986 Hydrocarbon Law, made it possible for foreign capital to be employed in enhanced oil recovery (EOR) schemes in fields already in operation. After extremely long negotiations, such a contract was finally signed in February 1996 between Sonatrach and Arco for EOR to be used in the Rhourde El Baguel field as part of a 25-year production-sharing agreement. This field is old (it was discovered in 1962), and had had a relatively low recovery rate of some 20 per cent. The plan involves a combination of gas injection and some in-fill drilling to double the recovery rate, adding 0.5 billion barrels to reserves. In terms of incremental production, the target is to transform a pre-EOR production rate of just 20 thousand b/d to 125 thousand b/d after 2000, with an intermediate post-EOR plateau of 50 thousand b/d. Arco received its first equity production from the development in November 1996.[3] It should be noted that this is just the first of a series of potential EOR developments, and so taking a longer time span, the potential increment from such deals is far more than the 100 thousand b/d from the Arco deal alone.

Before addressing the question of the overall rise in Algerian production, the question of pipeline infrastructure and capacity needs to be addressed. Figure 4.4 shows a schemata for the main constituents of the Algerian system. The binding constraint is the maximum volume that can reach the coast for refinery use or for export, and is the sum of the capacities of the OZ1, OB1 and OK1 pipelines as shown in Figure 4.4, together with the OT1 route through Tunisia. The current combined capacity of these routes, (expected to remain largely unchanged through to 2000), is 76.5 tonnes per year (1.65 million b/d). The OT1 pipeline runs at far below its capacity, and given its position is largely irrelevant in terms of the main sources of incremental production. Ignoring OT1, we then have an evacuation capacity of 62.5 million tonnes, of which (net of OT1 shipments) about

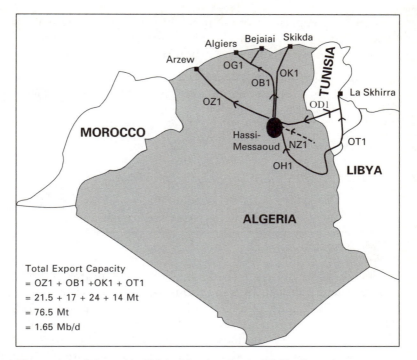

Total Export Capacity
= OZ1 + OB1 +OK1 + OT1
= 21.5 + 17 + 24 + 14 Mt
= 76.5 Mt
= 1.65 Mb/d

Figure 4.4: Schemata of Main Algerian Crude Oil Pipelines

40 million tonnes are utilised as of 1997. This leaves spare capacity of 22.5 million tonnes (500 thousand b/d), which we would estimate is split between the pipelines as follows; OB1 10 million tonnes, OK1 9 million tonnes, and OZ1 3.5 million tonnes. Apart from the potential for local bottlenecks (as noted above, the development of Qoubba in particular raises pipeline issues), spare pipeline capacity for incremental production, net of declines from existing fields not subject to EOR, does not appear to represent any immediately binding constraint.

In all, the addition of the Hassi Berkine area with the EOR projects and other fields, net of the reduction in the output of existing fields, brings a net gain of some 0.4 million b/d up to 2005 from the trough in output that was shown in Figure 4.2. While a major increase for Algeria, this is rather minor on a world scale. The extent to which the oil production increase leads to trade flow changes depends in large part on the role of condensates. Algeria is predominately a gas province, with a high condensate potential. To illustrate, Table 4.6 shows the breakdown of Algerian hydrocarbon reserves as of 1998.

Table 4.6: Algerian Hydrocarbon Reserves. 1998. Million Barrels of Oil Equivalent.

	Mboe	*Per Cent*
Crude Oil	9,720	27
Condensate	3,240	9
LPG	2,520	7
Natural Gas	20,520	57
Total	36,000	100

Source: Sonatrach

The division between crude oil and condensates is both arbitrary and political. In trade terms, the distinction between, say, extra production of a 47° API crude oil stream and a 51° API condensate stream is largely irrelevant. Currently very little, about 3 per cent, of condensate is blended into the crude oil stream with almost all condensate production going for export. Further out, one variable is the plan for the construction of a 120 thousand b/d condensate refinery, and the associated potential for the diversion of crude oil into the export stream.

The total volume increase may be small, but in terms of the Mediterranean market, incremental low sulphur supplies from a supplier, proximate to the market, is of significance. The increase also represents a sharp rise in Algeria's exportable surplus. As we have already noted that the Mediterranean has a sulphur and fuel oil problem in refining, Algerian oil has a natural regional market. Algeria, while once a major exporter to the USA, is now almost exclusively a regional crude oil supplier.

Table 4.7 shows Algerian crude oil exports by destination since 1980. Note how wedded Algeria is to the European downstream system. Penetration into the US market was lost in the early 1980s (except today for a continuing market in condensates, not covered with the OPEC definition of crude oil as used in the data shown in Table 4.7). Exports to the USA of

Table 4.7: Algerian Crude Oil Exports and Destination. 1980–97. Thousand Barrels per Day

	80	85	90	91	92	93	94	95	96	97	98
Europe	280.5	231.8	263.4	334.8	269.9	265.3	288.7	283.3	320.9	305.9	338.0
of which											
France	99.3	27.5	50.2	70.7	65.1	62.1	81.1	94.7	78.2	101.6	103.8
Germany	96.7	20.5	50.0	36.4	53.0	75.2	84.0	25.8	45.1	-	36.0
Italy	16.3	70.4	90.2	108.7	90.2	71.8	63.5	77.4	94.5	84.7	102.0
Netherlands	8.9	21.7	10.0	44.2	3.9	3.3	-	1.9	-	2.9	8.7
Spain	21.5	20.3	9.1	14.3	10.8	9.7	11.4	13.1	18.6	23.8	31.1
UK	4.7	17.2	4.4	18.2	26.4	23.8	15.4	10.1	20.7	8.0	14.0
USA	414.2	16.9	5.2	-	-	-	1.7	1.6	-	-	13.8*
Canada	-	7.0	-	-	3.3	21.7	31.4	41.0	63.8	59.7	66.7
Other	29.8	22.5	13.0	9.9	11.8	27.0	16.9	16.8	6.1	7.5	6.7
TOTAL	715.5	272.0	280.6	344.7	279.4	308.0	329.2	332.8	390.8	373.1	425.2

* 1998 exports to USA corrected from error in source

Source: OPEC *Annual Statistical Bulletin*, various issues

414 thousand b/d in 1980 have been negligible in the 1990s. Apart from in recent years the exploitation of a niche market for delivery into Canada, as would be expected Algeria is heavily reliant on Italy and France for a market. Given the general trends of export flows from Latin America and elsewhere into the US Gulf Coast, the prospects for any resumption of significant Algerian trade outside the Mediterranean remain limited.

4. Egypt

While Algerian production expands, the major challenge in Egypt by contrast lies in maintaining current levels. Egyptian oil production comes from four main areas: the Gulf of Suez (some 80 per cent), the Western Desert (about 9 per cent), the Eastern Desert (around 6 per cent) and the Sinai Peninsula (about 5 per cent). As Figure 4.5 demonstrates, after a decade of increase, production peaked in 1996 at close to 925 thousand b/d, before falling back to 851 thousand b/d in 1999. The chances of any stabilisation of output depend on the extent to which new developments can offset the declines in ageing fields.

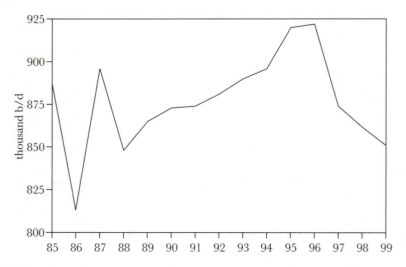

Figure 4.5: Egyptian Crude Oil Production. 1985–99. Thousand Barrels per Day

A state agency, the General Petroleum Authority, was established in 1956 and was later renamed the Egyptian General Petroleum Corporation (EGPC). In 1963, the government introduced a new policy of encouraging foreign companies to explore on a half share joint-venture basis with EGPC. In the same year, the national oil company concluded its first joint ventures with the International Egyptian Oil Company (the local affiliate of Italy's Agip), Amoco and Phillips Petroleum. A new petroleum policy was introduced in August 1973 which provided for the use of production-sharing agreements. In addition to supervising the entire Egyptian hydrocarbon exploration and production industry, EGPC has its own exploration and production activities through its General Petroleum Company (GPC) subsidiary. GPC accounts for only a small proportion of Egyptian oil output, but it explores actively in a number of regions, holding numerous exploration licences for acreages in the Sinai, the Gulf of Suez and the Western Desert. EGPC takes a 50 per cent stake in joint-venture operating companies that are created when an oil or gas discovery becomes a commercial development.

The split of output between producing companies is shown in Table 4.8, with the profile dominated by two main companies. The biggest producer is the Gulf of Suez Petroleum Company (GUPCO), a joint venture between Amoco and EGPC. GUPCO

Table 4.8: Egyptian Oil Production by Company. 1995–8. Barrels per Day

Company	1995	1996	1997	1998
GUPCO	380,420	352,320	326,740	323,300
Petrobel	237,440	219,740	201,460	200,080
Suco/Deoco	69,480	67,880	63,360	64,660
Agiba	49,020	47,200	47,580	49,260
Khalda	30,880	35,000	34,800	33,480
Qarun	300	11,260	33,620	36,160
GPC	26,960	27,040	29,620	33,740
Geisum	12,820	24,420	19,260	15,880
Bapetco	25,060	21,020	18,780	15,080
Zafco	16,720	16,760	14,640	12,360
Geptco (Petrozeit)	500	5,440	12,340	9,780
Other	39,120	27,600	25,200	26,440

Source: *Middle East Economic Survey,* various issues.

is the main producer in the Gulf of Suez basin, and although its output remains substantial it has been falling markedly in recent years. With new GUPCO developments heavily biased towards gas, there is little possibility of the steady decline in GUPCO's oil production being rapidly halted.

The second most important producer is Petrobel, a joint venture between EGPC and a subsidiary of ENI, the International Egyptian Oil Company (IEOC). Like GUPCO, Petrobel production, primarily from the mature Belayim and Ras Gharib fields, is in decline. The company's twelve development leases were re-negotiated in 1997, enabling Petrobel to boost its exploration activities. IEOC is planning to spend around $1 billion over the next five years on exploration and the development of oil and gas discoveries concentrated mainly in the Sinai, the Delta and offshore Mediterranean. A total of $1.7 billion has already been spent on the Belayim Land and Marine fields in the Gulf of Suez, but as yet new developments have not impacted on the rapid decline in production.

The pattern has emerged of concentration on gas by established large companies, and oil upstream becoming more weighted towards the smaller companies, in particular Apache, Seagull, Petra Oil (all American), Tullow Oil (Irish), Samsung, Yukong, (both Korean), Cabre Exploration (Canadian) and INA-Naftaplin (Croatian). The decline of 90 thousand b/d between 1995 and 1997 in GUPCO and Petrobel production has been partially offset by new streams from Apache and Seagull, operating smaller fields in the Western Desert. The Qarun block, for example, was producing 5 thousand b/d in 1995, but by 1997, this had risen to over 40 thousand b/d. In October 1997, Apache and Seagull made another major discovery in the Western Desert, in the East Beni Suef Concession, with some 100 million barrels of recoverable crude. Apache alone has made a total of fourteen discoveries in Egypt since 1994.

Apache has also acquired Mobil's interests in three exploration concessions in the Western Desert. The new acreage lies in between the Qarun and Khalda concessions, currently producing over 70 thousand b/d combined. Qarun is owned 75 per cent by Apache, which is also the operator, with Seagull having the remaining 25 per cent. The two are also partners in the East Beni Suef concession south of Cairo and the Darag offshore block at the northern end of the Gulf of Suez. Each holds 50 per cent in these two latter blocks, Seagull farming into them when it bought Global Natural Resources, of Houston, in 1996.

Both Apache and Seagull are also involved separately in various Egyptian concessions. The Khalda field is operated in joint venture with EGPC, the half share foreign ownership being owned 40 per cent by Apache, Repsol, the operator (50 per cent), and Samsung (10 per cent). Seagull has 100 per cent interests in the East Zeit permit offshore in the Gulf of Suez, and also in the South Hurghada block onshore south of the Gulf of Suez, and in the west Abu al-Gharadiq concession, west of Cairo in the Western Desert.

Egypt continues to report a steady stream of new oil discoveries, both in established producing regions, such as the Gulf of Suez, and in newer, less explored areas, such as the Western desert and Offshore Mediterranean. Whilst these new finds are modest for the most part, they at least have the effect of maintaining the underlying reserve base at a relatively stable level. Most discoveries are gas, although a series of oil finds have been made, as is shown in Table 4.9.

Egypt's plans for the development of its domestic oil industry are integrated with the natural gas sector. The government is seeking to slow the rate of decline in its mature oilfields whilst developing its natural gas reserves and the use of that gas in the domestic market. Changes made to PSAs in 1986 (which gave companies the rights to the gas they discovered), coupled with the increases introduced in 1998 in the price paid by the government to producers, have stimulated interest in Egyptian gas. By increasing the use of natural gas domestically, the government aims to slow the rate of growth in consumption of oil products, thereby maximising volumes of crude oil available for export.

In terms of developing the oil sector, the priorities include further attracting foreign capital for crude oil exploration projects. The strategy for attracting companies has been implemented by improving the terms for small and marginal field developments, particularly in the Western Desert and offshore Mediterranean. A joint committee has been formed,

Table 4.9: Egyptian Oil Discoveries. 1996–1998

Concession	Region	Test Flow	Date of Discovery	Company
North October	Gulf of Suez	6,000	98	GUPCO
North October	Gulf of Suez	1,616	98	GUPCO
South Gharib	Gulf of Suez	19,400	98	EGPC-Amoco
South Gharib	Gulf of Suez	8,000	98	EGPC-Amoco
East Tanka	Gulf of Suez	10,600	98	EGPC-Amoco
North Tuly	Gulf of Suez	6,000	98	Pennzoil
Ashrafi	Gulf of Suez	4,000	98	Agiba (EGPC/IEOC)
South Geisum	Gulf of Suez	768	98	Geisum Petroleum (Egypt)
Belayim Marine	Gulf of Suez	2,000	98	Petrobel
Belayim Marine	Gulf of Suez	414	98	Petrobel
West Ish al Malaka	Gulf of Suez	1,500	98	Coplex
W Med (Block 1)	West of Alexandria	8,500	98	Apache/Repsol
East Beni Suef	Astride Nile, South of Cairo	9,200	98	Apache/Seagull (US)
East Beni Suef	Astride Nile, South of Cairo	2,100	98	Apache/Seagull
Qarun	Western Desert	1,200	98	Apache/Seagull
South Dabaa	Western Desert	2,341	98	HBS (Tunisia)
South Dabaa	Western Desert	2,500	98	HBS
South Dabaa	Western Desert	4,500	98	HBS
South Dabaa	Western Desert	5,680	98	HBS
South Dabaa	Western Desert	1,200	98	HBS
Meleika	Western Desert	900	98	Petrobel
Meleika	Western Desert	1,302	98	Petrobel
Ras al Qattana	Western Desert	800	98	Petrobel
Khalda	Western Desert	1,160	98	Repsol
Qarun	Western Desert	518	98	Qarun(Apache/EGPC/ Seagull)
Block 1 West Med	West of Alexandria	8,277	98	Apache/Repsol/Amoco
West 'Ish al-Mallaha	Onshore, West of Gulf of Suez	6,805	97	Cabre (Can)/Coplex (Egypt)
East Tanka	Gulf of Suez	11,000	97	GUPCO
East Shuqair	Gulf of Suez	5,000	97	GUPCO
Belayim Marine	Gulf of Suez	960	97	Petrobel
Ras Garra	Gulf of Suez	17,000	97	Petrobel
East Beni Suef	South of Cairo	7,000	97	Seagull/Apache
Kenz (Khalda)	Western Desert	9,205	97	Khalda
Wadi El Rayan	Western Desert	1,764	97	Apache
North Qaran	Western Desert	1,950	97	Apache
East Tanka Marine	Gulf of Suez	4,884	96	GUPCO

Table 4.9: *continued*

Concession	Region	Test Flow	Date of Discovery	Company
East Tanka Marine	Gulf of Suez	800	96	GUPCO
Ashrafi	Gulf of Suez	4,000	96	Petrobel
Belayim	Gulf of Suez	1,000	96	Petrobel
Belayim	Gulf of Suez	2,516	96	Petrobel
Ras Qattara	Western Desert	1,700	96	Petrobel
West Abu al-Gharadiq	Western Desert	5,035	96	Petrobel/Seagull/INA Naftaplin
Burg al-'Arab	Western Desert	1,500	96	Gharib (Egypt)
Deep Meleiha	Western Desert	9,575	96	Petrobel
Abu Sannan	Western Desert	500	96	GPC (Egypt)
Qarun	Western Desert	3,700	96	Apache
SW Qarun	Western Desert	950	96	Apache

Source: *Middle East Economic Survey*, various issues.

which is designed to allow for the exchange of information between companies. As a result, new entrants do not have to start afresh in old concessions, but can build on previous information. The Egyptian Oil Ministry also allows companies that make small discoveries to use nearby surface facilities and infrastructure, thereby minimising front-end investment costs. Meanwhile, private Egyptian companies are also being encouraged to participate. In 1997, the first oilfield with a majority Egyptian private sector shareholding went into regular production.

Most oil development work is taking place in producing areas, as the replacement of reserves has been carried out by the use of 3D seismic imaging and processing techniques, horizontal drilling and enhanced oil recovery (EOR). These efforts have focused on arresting decline rates of mature reservoirs. In some places, field facilities have been unitised to encourage the development of marginal discoveries. In recent years, both GUPCO and Petrobel have had discoveries in areas within or directly adjacent to their existing production. Their activities also include expanded development and extensive EOR projects involving both gas lift and water injection.

Official Egyptian policy has been to maintain oil production at close to 900 thousand b/d. To achieve this, operators have been encouraged to develop all commercial finds, even small ones, as quickly as possible. Development activity is beginning to pick up again, after a lull which reflected a drop in the discovery rate in the early 1990s. New fields continue to come on stream, but they tend to be small. Meanwhile, exploration efforts are steadily yielding modest finds, which have the effect of keeping the remaining reserve base relatively stable.

In sum, Egypt should not be expected to make significant incremental additions to the Mediterranean supply balance within the time-frame of this study. New discoveries are being made, but mature fields are experiencing declining production, albeit delayed by the use of enhanced recovery techniques. The Egyptian government's aim to increase the domestic consumption of natural gas in order to free up crude for export to the Mediterranean basin is not yet producing the kind of rising substitution rate which was hoped for.

Proven gas reserves in the Nile Delta and Western Desert have increased by 400 per cent from 1981 to the present level of 31.5 trillion cubic feet (tcf). A significant proportion of recently discovered reserves are due on stream quickly, and are already contracted to the domestic market. The solution to the potential problem might be to aggressively develop gas export markets in the Mediterranean, albeit into a European market where prices are beginning to weaken significantly. Thus, while Egypt remains a significant crude oil producer in the Mediterranean region, it is in the export of gas where the greatest attention and resources are now being channelled, and where Egypt and the major foreign companies involved in the Egyptian energy sector see its greatest potential for future growth.

5.   Syria

With severe difficulties in maintaining current production levels, and with consumption rising fast, Syria's major problem is to even maintain net exporter status. Having become a net exporter only in 1987, Syria now faces a prolonged period during which the export surplus will be gradually whittled away.

As is shown in Figure 4.6, Syrian oil production underwent a dramatic surge in the later half of the 1980s following the development of a series of major finds, and reached 610

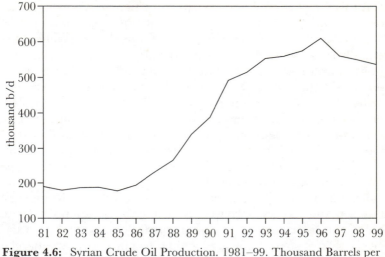

Figure 4.6: Syrian Crude Oil Production. 1981–99. Thousand Barrels per Day

thousand b/d in 1996. However, this might now be seen as the effective peak in Syrian production, as field maturity has set in. Many Syrian fields are in need of enhanced recovery methods in order to stem the imminent decline. Although production was given a boost towards the end of 1994 when the Deir ez-Zor Petroleum Company (DEZPC) brought its Jafra (15 thousand b/d) and Qahar (30 thousand b/d) fields on stream, the further development of new fields has stalled in recent years. Current production stands at 550 thousand b/d, with few new fields under development. The reserve base is very heavily concentrated in a few key fields, most notably, Soudie (1 billion barrels), Karatchok (200–400 mb), Omar North (200 mb), Al-Thayyem (180 mb), Jbeisseh (150 mb) and Rumailan (115 mb).

The current structure of the industry was laid down in 1973, when it was decided that the Syrian General Petroleum Company should be divided into five operating companies, all state-owned and attached to the Ministry of Petroleum and Mineral Resources. The Syrian Petroleum Company (SPC) is responsible for all upstream operations: exploration, field development and production. The Homs Refinery Company and the Banias Oil Refining Company operate Syria's two refineries. The Syrian Company for Oil Transport (SCOT) controls the country's domestic pipeline network, which carries oil from the fields in the north-east to the refineries and the Tartus and Banias oil terminals. Meanwhile, domestic marketing and distribution is the responsibility of the Syrian Company for Storage and Distribution of Petroleum Products (Mahruqat). A separate organisation, Sytrol, handles the export of crude oil.

In 1974 the government launched an open door policy designed to encourage international companies to engage in oil exploration and development in Syria. An area of 25 thousand km^2 was reserved for SPC and the remaining 50 thousand km^2 of oil acreage were assigned under the terms of service-type agreements with foreign contractors. The first service contract concluded with a foreign company was signed with Rompetrol in 1974, and several more were signed in the period up to 1980. Some of those contractors subsequently relinquished their tracts either totally or partially after failing to make any commercial discoveries. However, on a 15,750 km^2 acreage in the Deir ez-Zor region, awarded in July 1977 to Samoco and Deminex, a series of major finds were made in the mid 1980s, but only after Samoco had withdrawn in 1982 and sold its 65 per cent stake to Pecten (which became operator) and its parent company Shell.

There are four significant producers of crude oil in Syria. The dominant force is the Al-Furat Petroleum Company (AFPC), a joint venture established in May 1985 between the state-owned Syrian Petroleum Company and three foreign companies, Royal Dutch/Shell, its affiliate Pecten Syria Petroleum and Deminex. The AFPC's fields in the north east of the country, in particular in the Deir ez-Zor region, currently produce approximately 350 thousand b/d of high quality light crude. At Al-Thayyem, output has declined notably in recent years from a peak of 80 thousand b/d in 1991 to around 45 thousand b/d today. The Omar/Omar North field came on stream in 1989, producing 55 thousand b/d, but following an intervention by a government wishing to boost output, some serious reservoir damage was caused. The AFPC has developed 32 fields to date. In the last period of new field development, six came on stream in 1992, and a further two in 1993, but none at all in the next five years.

The second major company is the Syrian Petroleum Company (SPC) itself, whose production, from fields in the Soudie-

Karatchok region and at Jbeissah in the north east of the country, reached a peak in the late 1970s when output exceeded 165 thousand barrels per day. The decline in production has been modest but continuous since then, although a more or less constant 140 thousand b/d has been achieved in recent years. The crude produced from these fields is heavy and extremely sour (between 18° and 24° API gravity, 3.8–4.2 per cent sulphur). SPC is also involved in a joint venture with Elf Aquitaine, known as the Deir ez-Zor Petroleum Company (DEZPC), and a fourth group is led by the Irish company Tullow Oil.

The spate of oil discoveries made in the 1980s by the Shell and Deminex group in the Deir ez-Zor region of eastern Syria triggered a sudden upsurge in oil exploration and development activity, and encouraged a number of other foreign companies to enter the sector. Several held exploration licences, but subsequently withdrew after failing to make commercial discoveries. Out of the thirteen exploration licences awarded to twelve foreign contractors between 1987 and 1990, eleven were relinquished within seven years.

During the 1990s, there has been a dearth in the number of licences awarded to foreign companies and the Syrian upstream has stagnated. However, despite the failure of most of the foreign companies that acquired exploration licences in the late 1980s, exploration activity has continued. However, activity is slight, and production declines are becoming precipitous.

6. Italy

Italy is by far the smallest of the five major regional producers, and developments are not yet of sufficient scale for Italy to overtake Syria in the medium term. However, there are developments sufficient to push Italy's production to some 350 thousand barrels per day. Moreover, this is to the largest part medium and high quality crude oil, rather than the ultra heavy crude normally associated with Italian fields, and it is close to market. In other words the incremental production will cut Italy's supply deficit barrel for barrel. Each new barrel of production compounds the effect on the regional balance of the weakening of Italian demand arising from substitution away from fuel oil.

Figure 4.7 shows the current areas of production and exploration activity in Italy. Exploration began in the mid-1940s in the Po Valley, which proved to be mainly a gas-bearing region. In the first forty years of exploration, while some twenty oilfields were discovered, none of these earlier fields were particularly significant. In the 1970s, exploration effect was extended into the Adriatic. The movement offshore saw Elf find oil in 1974 south east of Bari. The next year the Rospo Mare field was found, producing a particularly foul crude oil of just 12° API gravity. This achievement was crowned in 1979 with the discovery of the Sarago Mare field. At 8° API gravity,

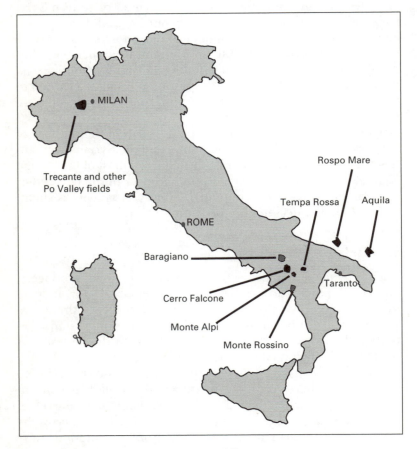

Figure 4.7: Italian Producing Areas and Prospects

this is one of the few fields where water injection would drive the oil *down*, and a strong contender for the worst quality commercial oil in the world. Compared with the 28 producing wells Elf lavished on Rospo Mare, it is perhaps not surprising that one was thought quite enough for Sarago Mare.

By the mid-1980s, the Italian upstream was weak. In 1984, production (including condensate) stood at about 40 thousand b/d. Of the eleven fields producing more than 500 b/d, other than one condensate field all had oil with a gravity of 24° API or below, and six of the eleven were 14° API or below. Italy had acquired the reputation of being the producer of small amounts of treacle, an oil province where the most useful piece of extraction equipment was a spoon.

The reputation may have stuck, but the nature of the Italian upstream changed with two significant finds in the 1980s. In 1984 ENI found the Trecate field in the Po Valley. This has represented the mainstay of Italian production, with a 1996 production level of some 67 thousand b/d of 43° API crude oil. Then in 1988 came the first significant find in the southern Italian onshore, the Monte Alpi field.

The Monte Alpi discovery created the climate for the southern Appennine region to become a genuine exploration hotspot. The exploration has been led primarily by ENI, Enterprise and LASMO, with the involvement, *inter alia*, of Mobil, BG, Petrofina and Union Texas. Three main fields have been found to date around Val d'Agri. The first of these, Monte Alpi (60 per cent ENI, and 40 per cent Enterprise), started limited production of 39° API gravity oil in 1993, and, as discussed below, now awaits an evacuation route for significant production to begin. The second is Cerro Falcone (55 per cent Enterprise, 45 per cent ENI), where appraisal wells have produced 32° API gravity oil. The third is Tempa Rossa, originally discovered by Petrofina, but which extends into a licence area held by a consortium, originally led by LASMO, which also involves Enterprise, Mobil and Petrofina. Tempa Rossa is closer to the reputation of Italian oil, with test wells showing oil of 20° API gravity. In all three fields the geology is fairly complex, with a large oil-bearing column (750 metres at Cerro Falcone, 1100 metres at Tempa Rossa).

The southern Appennines is a remote and inaccessible

mountainous area. Design and implementation of a pipeline has then been the major logistical problem in its development. To date, Monte Alpi production has been moved by truck to the ENI refinery at Taranto, and production has therefore been limited. Full development involves the construction of a pipeline to Taranto, to take the output of Cerro Falcone, Monte Alpi and Tempa Rossa. The likely capacity of this line would be in the region of about 200 thousand b/d, i.e. almost twice the level of Italy's current crude oil production.

Outside Val d'Agri, exploration continues in the Adriatic off Bari, and the Po Valley is not played out as an oil region. However, Val d'Agri remains the focus of attention. Given the current timetable for Val d'Agri development, plus a modicum of success in other exploration, the incremental output from Italy in a base case could be expected to be of the order of 250 thousand barrels over the next decade. While not dramatic globally, this would still represent a significant increment in the Mediterranean context, particularly in view of the relative stasis in all the other major Mediterranean producers bar Algeria.

Notes

1. Estimates of costs place the total at $4.30 per barrel, i.e. a development cost of $1.30 per barrel, operating costs of $2.50 per barrel and additional overheads of 50 cents per barrel. Salomon Brothers reported in *Middle East Economic Survey*, 10 February 1997.

2. Nezla is a 30 inch pipeline with capacity of 350 thousand barrels per day. See *Middle East Economic Survey*, 23/30 December 1996. The pipeline is shown in Figure 4.4 as the route NZ1.

3. The other fields where Sonatrach has indicated a desire to use EOR contracts are Hassi Messaoud, El Gassi, Ben Kahla, Haoud Berkaoui, El Adeb Larache and Zarzaitine, together with the oil rings within the Rhourde Nouss and Hassi R'Mel gas fields.

5 THE PROXIMATE OIL PRODUCERS: THE CASPIAN AND IRAQ

1. Introduction

On the supply side of the Mediterranean market, we have grouped changes in production into three categories. The first, as considered in the previous chapter, is changes in indigenous production, i.e. in those countries we have classified on the demand side as being Mediterranean because of their source of crude oil. The second category is those countries who do or will place oil directly into the Mediterranean, and have limited flexibility in diverting it. This consists of part of the production of Iraq, the Caspian area and of Russia. The third category is a derived balancing item of Middle East, North Sea and West African crude. This represents oil which currently flows into the Mediterranean, whether through the Straits of Gibraltar or through the Sumed pipeline, which would be displaced by any increases in the sum of the first two categories relative to total regional demand.

This chapter considers the second of these categories of producer, those which can be called proximate suppliers into the Mediterranean market. For these countries supplies enter the region simply because that is what their oil infrastructure logistics dictate, and they have little discretion in choosing between northern and southern Europe, or between western and eastern markets, according to market conditions. In the context of the Mediterranean this is, for example, what distinguishes Iraq from Saudi Arabia. The latter is a substantial supplier into the Mediterranean through the Sumed pipeline as was detailed in Chapter 1. However, Saudi Arabia uses a market allocation policy, optimises between regions and represents, de facto, a form of swing producer into the Mediterranean. Should circumstances so impel it, it is not compelled to supply oil into the region. By contrast, as described further below, Iraq has a very limited ability to swing between regions following the dictates of varying regional circumstances. The amount of its oil that enters the region is not directly determined by pull factors of regional imbalances. It is in that sense that we give separate consideration to Iraq and not to Saudi Arabia within the context of the Mediterranean. Iraqi flows create direct regional displacements, while Saudi flows play a more accommodatory role.

We concentrate in this chapter on the Caspian and Iraq, considered in turn in the next two sections within the context of their impact on the Mediterranean. We give these two areas particular consideration as they are the two that have attracted the greatest hyperbole in terms of their future potential. While we tend to cast a dampener across most of that potentiality, the importance of these two areas at the margin, in perception if not in reality, exists in a form that is not shared by the Russian oil industry.

Despite that prescription, Russia is of central importance. Russia is the heart of negotiations for the development and transit of Caspian oil, and has played a leading edge role in the jockeying for position in Iraq. Within the context of the Mediterranean market, the Russian Black Sea ports are an important outlet for both crude oil and oil products into the region. Further, should the Russian oil industry rebound and its export infrastructure expand, then that would have a major impact on regional balances.

There are, at the extremes, two possibilities. The first is the status quo, a Russian industry where the export potential from the Black Sea ports continues to be constrained by bottlenecks and organisational failure, and where production continues to be static or falling in the face of political failure and under-investment. The alternative is Russia redux, with production climbing and running ahead of oil demand.

Our approach to the Caspian issues is based on the former scenario on Russia, and this requires some brief justification. The crisis in Russia is demonstrated by the path of oil production and consumption in the Russian Federation since 1985, as shown in Figure 5.1. The first feature to note is that the declines in both series have different roots. The sharp falls began after 1991, and reflect the collapse of Russian GDP, the sharp rise in the domestic price of energy and the sectoral collapse of energy-intensive heavy industries. In just seven years demand was reduced by 2.6 million b/d, a fall of over 50 per cent.

While the path of demand is related to the overall economic

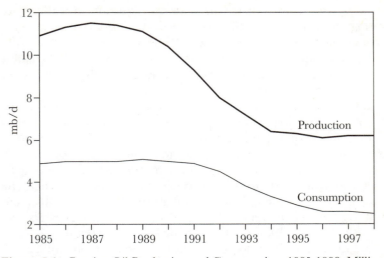

Figure 5.1: Russian Oil Production and Consumption. 1985-1998. Million Barrels per Day

performance, the path of supply has more sector specific roots. The fall in production began in 1989, before the break-up of the Soviet Union. Over the next six years Russian output fell by a staggering 5 million b/d, before entering a period of more gradual decline in the latter half of the 1990s. The seeds of this implosion were sown in the late 1970s and early 1980s, with under-investment in exploration and the development of new fields, combined with a system that encouraged overproduction beyond sustainable levels in existing reservoirs. When the decline came in the existing fields, it was thus far more severe, and the lack of investment meant that there was no new tranche of major fields to compensate for the decline.

The decline of Russian production would have happened regardless of the political or economic integrity of the Soviet Union. All that political disintegration and economic collapse added was a further layer of dislocations, for instance in sourcing spare parts, and a tightening of the already pronounced capital starvation of the industry. Indeed, some of the more florid Cold War histories have given the prospective production profile as seen from 1989 a key role in the unfolding of events. That may be going too far, but it is certainly true that key Kremlin decision-makers were aware of the path that oil output, and therefore foreign currency receipts, were irrevocably bound on. The most damaging mistakes within the oil industry were made in the Brezhnev, and not the Gorbachev, era, and it is to the greatest extent coincidental that at first sight the series shown in Figure 5.1 seem to fall together.

The collapse of the Soviet Union led to a break-up of the Soviet oil industry, resulting in a profusion of highly political companies with a dominant role played by Lukoil. It also led to a swift infusion of western capital, followed by a more gradual, and in the case of some companies, a painful retrenchment. A sector which needs massive investment has instead been the major source of domestic capital outflow from the Russian economy in recent years. We have considered investments and production possibilities at the field level. From this we have concluded that, for at least a decade, there is no possibility of a Russian oil industry spilling out to disturb the structure of flows within the Mediterranean market. In the medium term the key issue is not when will Russian production show a significant increase, but rather how much further it can fall in the interim.

2.   The Caspian

From the sheer volume of attention given to energy development in the Caspian region over the course of the 1990s, one might assume that it represents a watershed in the history of the oil market. The Caspian has been assigned a significance ranking it alongside the discovery of Spindletop, the development of Saudi Arabia, and the creation of the oil industries in the North Sea and Alaska. However, once the veneer of publicity has been scratched away, a rather different picture emerges. In short, within the broader picture of oil market development in the first decades of the next century, the Caspian is insignificant.

The division between the publicity and the reality may seem a puzzling one, until the role of international politics is accounted for. The Caspian has represented a prolonged and deliberate intervention by foreign policy concerns riding rough-shod over hard economics. The US government deliberately over-inflated expectations of the reserve base, and has then intervened constantly in the debate over transit routes, placing its policy concerns above the economic viability of the options available. A summary of American policy as 'Turkey good, Iran and Russia bad' is simplistic, but not overly so.

The aims of the USA have been summarised by the Presidential Advisor on energy developments in the region, Richard Morningstar, in Senate hearings.[1] Those aims are fourfold. First, to strengthen the independence of the Caspian states. Secondly, to mitigate conflicts by building links between the states. Thirdly, to bolster the energy security of the West by ensuring a free flow of oil and gas to the world market. Finally, to enhance commercial opportunities for US companies.

These aims demonstrate a raft of foreign policy concerns. They are also not entirely logical or consistent with other strands of US policy. On the first aim, strengthening the independence of the Caspian states is an obvious goal in order to reduce the ambit of Russian and Iranian influence. However, it sits uneasily with section 907 of the Freedom Support Act, which makes Azerbaijan not just the only former Soviet state to face US sanctions, but also the only country in the world where even humanitarian aid from the USA is illegal. The Armenian lobby in the USA is small, but highly effective.

The aim of conflict mitigation through Caspian oil is also questionable. There seems no obvious reason why conflict prevention in the area should be improved by pipelines and oil developments. Chechnya is no more stable today because it has a key pipeline running through it, and the roots of conflict between Armenia and Azerbaijan are more fundamental. Indeed, increasing economic interdependence through pipelines arguably just adds a further source of potential conflict.

Morningstar's third aim borders on the absurd. If the aim is to ensure a free world oil market, then that aim would be better served by immediately lifting sanctions against Iran and Libya than by tortuous long-run negotiations for a far smaller amount of oil. The subcontext is primarily a desire to diversify the sources of oil away from the Middle East, and in that regard the Caspian makes only a very modest long-term contribution. Indeed, one could argue that compared to cargoes of waterborne crude oil from the Middle East, Caspian oil delivered through fixed pipelines across unstable countries represents a distinct worsening of western energy security.

The fourth stated aim of US policy is also questionable, in that the Caspian does not represent the lowest cost way of achieving it. Part of the early attraction of the Caspian to US companies was that other and better commercial opportunities were blocked to them by the actions of their own government. US companies have been lobbying for many years for the opportunity to pursue commercial opportunities in Iran and Libya without that resulting in any positive movement on the part of government. Further, a major complaint of US companies in the Caspian is that the US government is attempting to impose uneconomic pipeline transit options on them, and in particular the $4 billion pipeline to Ceyhan in Turkey. Creating commercial opportunities is commendable, removing all the profit from those same opportunities for non-economic aims is somewhat less so, and completely blocking better opportunities represents plain obstruction.

The latter point was demonstrated starkly by a bizarre attack by John Wolf, Morningstar's successor as Presidential Advisor, against the main consortium operating in Azerbaijan.[2] Wolf complained that the consortium was not negotiating fast enough on the pipeline to Ceyhan. Whether such interference in a commercial negotiation reflects a commitment to the free market is a moot point. However, when commercial entities are negotiating a $4 billion project, the result is best left to those investors rather than the foreign policy concerns of government. When one of the worries of the investors is that there will not be enough oil to fill the pipeline, asking them to make a $4 billion leap of faith purely on the instinct of a government advisor represents a high level of government meddling. The above is simply to demonstrate that in the Caspian, politics has played a very strong role. The problems come when the economics take over.

A major part in the disinformation campaign has been the estimates of the reserve base of the Caspian region produced by the US Department of Energy. One version of these is shown in Table 5.1. The key figure is the estimate of 196 billion barrels for the total reserve base, a figure which has tended to be rounded up to 200 billion barrels. Once this figure was put in the public domain, and the confusion between the proven and possible elements left to continue, the perception of the Caspian as a new Saudi Arabia began to grow.

Table 5.1:   Proven and Possible Oil and Gas Reserves in Caspian Region.

	Oil Reserves (Billion Barrels)			Gas Reserves (Trillion cubic feet)		
	Proven	*Possible*	*Total*	*Proven*	*Possible*	*Total*
Azerbaijan	12.5	32	45	11	35	46
Kazakhstan	17.6	92	110	53–83	88	141–171
Turkmenistan	1.7	38	40	98–155	159	257–314
Uzbekistan	0.3	2	2	74–88	35	109–123
Total	32.1	164	196	236–337	317	553–654

Source: US Department of Energy

We have some major doubts as to the true size of the resource base. The 200 billion barrels figure has a long history in itself. It has various past incarnations as the estimate of the reserves of the Spratlys, of offshore China, of offshore Vietnam, of the Falklands, and of the Tarim basin. It seems that if one wishes to grab attention, a number within hailing distance of Saudi Arabia is called for. Yet the level of exploration success in the Caspian to date does not lend any credence to the parallel. As of 2000, proven reserves in the Caspian still fall short of the official US government figures for proven plus possible by an amount equal to about sixteen Prudhoe Bay fields. Thirty years of exploration worldwide have not yet produced a field to match Prudhoe Bay, and to suggest that exploration in the Caspian alone can rapidly deliver the equivalent of another sixteen seems to be stretching credulity to its absolute limit.

Our second source of doubt is pure economics. In a world with a natural tendency towards oil surplus, and with no foreseeable supply constraint, Caspian oil appears to be at best distinctly marginal, and more than likely uneconomic. At time of writing, the total of OPEC shut in capacity is about 10 per cent of the current world total capacity. On our estimates, even after a decade Caspian production will not reach half that level. The relatively high operating and capital costs in the Caspian are in fact a minor consideration, compared with the full rent sapping potential of the transit fees demanded by neighbouring countries.

The final source of doubt comes from tracking potential developments and output profiles, and adding in some realism about project timetables. As is detailed later in this section, this results in estimates of very little incremental production before 2005, and then a rise, primarily from Kazakhstan, in the period up to 2010. That rise is highly sensitive to further delay and can easily be pushed beyond 2010.

We would doubt the figure of 200 billion barrels of recoverable reserves on the grounds that either it is not there, or that it is not economic at current costs and current oil prices. There has been considerable political hyperbole over Caspian prospects, which conflicts sharply with the situation on, and in, the ground. The Caspian may be another North Sea in terms of resources, (but not potential production), but the common portrayal as another Saudi Arabia is highly exaggerated. Currently, as is seen below, only relatively small quantities of oil and gas are exported from Azerbaijan and Kazakhstan, a reflection of both the decline in production following independence in 1991, alongside the lack of transport facilities to the international market. The lack of export routes is, in turn, limiting the size of investments in the oil and gas sectors of Caspian region producers.

Any consideration of the export potential of the Caspian region brings us directly into the realm of international pipeline transit negotiations. The rules of the game are simple, just negotiate a route out, while minimising the political and economic leverage you inevitably hand to your neighbours, and trying to leave a non-zero netback to the wellhead net of all transit tariffs and transportation costs. Preferably, along the way this should be achieved in such a way as not to gain the enmity of the US government. After that, there is the matter of financing a multi-billion dollar long-term project. In other words, even large potential reserves do not necessarily translate into economically or politically viable trade flows, and the full development lags can be extremely long.

The major problem is pure geography. Figure 5.2 shows the geographical dilemmas posed by Caspian development, with two main areas of development being marked, namely offshore Azerbaijan and the Tengiz field in Kazakhstan. In terms of finding a pipeline route to a port, there are only three main options for the exit route for Caspian oil, plus one additional option for a purely land based movement to market. First, there

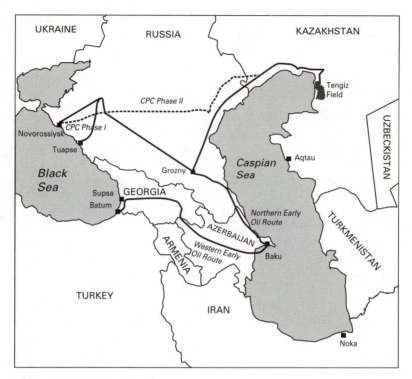

Figure 5.2: Caspian Pipelines

is the route to the Black Sea, and then through the Bosphorus into the Mediterranean. Secondly, there is a direct route to the Mediterranean via southern Turkey, and thirdly there is the route south towards the Gulf via Iran. A fourth, but now shelved, option arises from the possibility of moving oil eastwards across the vast plains of Kazakhstan and into China.

The essence of the Caspian problem is that all four of these broad routes suffer from political or economic problems, and sometimes both. The two longest routes (west towards southern Turkey or east towards China), carry extremely large capital costs. The route to the Black Sea has the drawback of increased reliance on Russia, combined with the severe problem of navigation through the Bosphorus and the Turkish reluctance to see any expansion of tanker movement through the hazardous and narrow channels. The routes through Iran face the problem of American opposition, and await a dramatic thawing in US–Iranian relations before they can become viable on any large scale.

i)   *Oil Development in Azerbaijan*

Azerbaijan is one of the oldest oil-producing regions in the world. The industry has been central to the Azerbaijan economy since the country became one of the major producers for the world market in the 1870s. It experienced its oil boom in the early 1900s, and its peak output level of 500 thousand b/d in the mid-1940s. In 1940, Azerbaijan's oil production amounted to 72 per cent of total FSU output, but by 1980, this figure had fallen to only 2 per cent. The legacy of the Soviet era and the many decades of oil production in the country is many mature fields and declining production, caused by inadequate investment and poor reservoir management techniques.

Azerbaijan's oil industry is a major factor underpinning the country's development programme. The investment climate is very favourable in comparison with the situation in other parts of the FSU, making it the biggest play so far for foreign companies. The so-called third oil era began in 1994, with the signing of the first major contract, the somewhat over-billed 'deal of the century', by the Azerbaijan International Operating Consortium (AIOC). For the foreign company operating in Azerbaijan, as with other parts of the Caspian region, risks still exist. Of particular importance in the context of Azeri oil are three factors.

First, there is the question of the status of the Caspian Sea, with the legal difference between a sea and an inland lake. The protracted dispute over whether the resources of the Caspian should be developed in common, or by each littoral state in its own sector, needs resolution before Azerbaijan can begin to be reconstructed as a major oil province. Secondly, there is Nagorno Karabakh, the disputed territory over which Azerbaijan fought a bloody war with Armenia between 1992 and 1994. Since 1994, the situation has been one of stalemate, but the underlying disputes have not been resolved. Prospects for a peace settlement are currently remote, and some sporadic fighting continues in border areas. The Karabakh Armenians occupy approximately

20 per cent of Azeri territory, and are well armed, highly organised and motivated. With oil revenues due to begin accruing to Baku, alarm is being voiced in Karabakh about the future Azeri potential to recommence hostilities in a bid to regain the lost area. As noted above, Azerbaijan also continues to suffer the loss of US financial aid, under the provisions of Section 907 of the US Freedom Support Act of 1992, as a result of its stance towards Armenia and the strength of the well organised and effective Armenian political lobby in the USA.

The third issue is Abkhazia and Georgia. Georgia is central to both the short-term and future export options for Azeri oil. Abkhazia fought a war for independence from Georgia between 1992 and 1993, and the question of the future relations between the two states remains unresolved. The relevance of the issue for Azeri oil is the proximity of the disputed area to the current rail export route to the Georgian port of Batum on the Black Sea, and to a planned pipeline route to Supsa, also on Georgia's Black Sea coast.

Since 1994 a series of consortia have been formed and production-sharing contracts signed. Here we focus on the three main current consortia. The first consortium to become involved in the Azeri oil industry was AIOC, led by BP Amoco with minor shares in the hands of ten other companies. It was created in 1994 to operate a production-sharing agreement for the Azeri, Chirag and deep water Guneshli fields, which hold an estimated 4 billion barrels of light, sweet crude. The fields were discovered in the 1980s, but development was delayed, primarily due to technological deficiencies. Peak production of around 650 thousand b/d is scheduled, which will be brought onshore just south of Baku, with a total investment scheduled to exceed $10 billion.

Whilst the AIOC is exploring known fields, the other blocks let out to foreign consortia have been for exploration acreage. The Caspian International Petroleum Company, (CIPCO) is primarily an Italo-Russian consortium led by Agip and Lukoil, with a further major share held by Pennzoil. CIPCO's agreement covers the Karabakh structure, with estimated possible reserves of up to 1 billion barrels.

The first of the groups to achieve any major exploration success has been the Shakh Deniz consortium, led by BP Amoco and Statoil. The production-sharing agreement was signed in June 1996, and three years later the consortium found a large gas and condensate accumulation in the offshore Shakh Deniz structure. The modern stage of exploration in offshore Azerbaijan is in too early a stage to draw firm conclusions. However, there are two ways at looking at the Shakh Deniz find. On the one hand it confirmed the presence of further offshore hydrocarbons, after a period when confidence had been reduced by a series of dry holes. On the other hand, it is a major gas and not oil discovery, and early estimates put possible crude oil reserves at Shakh Deniz at up to 3 billion barrels. The earlier hyperbole on offshore Caspian Sea development had been as an oil producer, while the early indications suggest a prolific gas prone region.

Azerbaijan was one of the first areas in the world where offshore fields were developed. The key early discovery was the giant Oil Rocks field (Neft Dashlary) in 1949. Guneshli was the next major discovery, coming onstream in 1980, and representing the bulk of total Azeri output through to the late 1990s. The offshore has been the focus of intensive exploration activity in recent years, with a series of major oil and gas prospects being discovered, including the Azeri, Chirag and Kyapaz fields, in a trend extending south east from Baku into increasingly deep water, along the Apsheron Sill structure, which stretches across the Caspian Sea to Turkmenistan. The Azeri government has been particularly interested in securing western involvement in the development of these more distant and difficult structures.

There are currently seventeen offshore fields producing, with Guneshli and Oil Rocks (Neft Dashlary) being the two main producers. The Oil Rocks development has accounted for approximately 40 per cent of cumulative production to date. Crude quality is generally light and sweet. The majority of offshore production so far has come from the shallow fields near the coast, as the deeper waters have prevented the development of more distant prospects. Recent indications from seismic data are that it is to the south of the Apsheron Sill structure in the waters towards Iran, rather than in the northern Caspian, that any giant fields may be found.

Most onshore fields were discovered some time ago, and

exploration in onshore regions has been declining throughout the past twenty years, although onshore fields have still contributed the majority of Azeri production to date. The current status of the onshore industry is much worse than that of the offshore sector. Prospective trends at depths greater than 3 thousand metres do remain however, having been ignored thus far, due to inadequate technology and capital. Azerbaijan's future production prospects well into the twenty-first century are thus centred on the offshore, and in particular on bringing Guneshli, Chirag and Azeri fields onstream.

To this point of time it has been a matter of managing a declining industry. As is shown in Figure 5.3, a rise in production in the 1980s stalled after 1987, and it was only in 1998 that the production level began to recover. Despite delays in transportation and difficulties at certain key fields, production increased in 1998 to 230 thousand barrels per day. Due to the continuing decline in domestic consumption, exports began to rise two years earlier, but it has taken more than a decade for output or exports to threaten to regain their 1980s peak levels. The main impetus for production in 1998 was the start-up in late 1997 of the 105 thousand b/d capacity Baku-Novorossiysk pipeline. Azeri crude

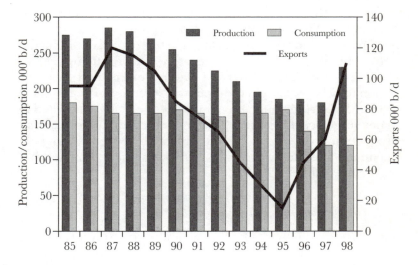

Figure 5.3: Azeri Crude Oil Production, Consumption and Exports. 1985–98. Thousand Barrels per Day

is piped to the Russian border, where Transneft takes over, and the Azeris receive an equivalent volume of Urals crude out of Novorossiysk. AIOC acts as shipper of the Azeri crude, and has priority access to send up to 100 thousand b/d through the pipeline.

A fundamental shift in perspective has occurred among oil companies in Baku in recent years, away from that of securing world prices in western markets, and towards getting the oil to whatever the most appropriate or economical market may be within the particular time-frame. With this in mind, it can no longer be assumed that Azeri crude, despite appearing to be deprived of a range of export options, will naturally gravitate towards the Mediterranean. Within the current time period before a main export pipeline becomes operational, a range of makeshift options, including swaps with Iran, are making themselves appealing to companies who wish to seize an opportunity to secure whatever revenues they can. Iran, for example, has a capacity for about 800 thousand b/d of Caspian crude. The Black Sea could also absorb a large supply increment, with its refining capacity vastly exceeding domestic demand for products.

The key characteristic of development timetables for Caspian projects is that they change rapidly, and almost always go backwards. When incremental production happens in discrete, large parts, this means that tracking the future path of production is fraught with difficulty. However, we have attempted that exercise on the basis of current Azeri projects, and found no reason to believe that Azeri output will serve as any major shock to the Mediterranean market, let alone the global market. The major surge occurs towards 2010, but on current information a production level of just over 1 million b/d seems about the maximum feasible, with a further rise to some 1.5 million b/d occurring well after 2010.

ii)   Oil Development in Kazakhstan

Kazakhstan's economic development aspirations rest largely on the success of the oil and gas industry for their fruition, and in particular on a large and fairly rapid increase in production. However, several factors have in the past mitigated against the achievement of this goal, and still threaten the speed of development of the Kazakhstan oil industry. Among the most basic of these obstacles is that Kazakhstan is of course a landlocked country, without direct access to world markets, and with an inefficient pipeline infrastructure which is not dedicated to exports beyond Russia.

Figure 5.4 shows the path of Kazakh crude oil production, consumption and exports. As in the case of Azerbaijan, exports have been rising in recent years, but have been driven more by falls in domestic demand than by any major expansion of productive capacity. The 1990s have been a decade of first managing decline, and then slowly beginning to regain past peaks. The major expansion is due later, with the main hope for future exports being the Tengiz field and the Caspian Pipeline Consortium (CPC), whose pipeline has been the subject of tortuous negotiations and numerous delays.

Reserve figures for the Former Soviet Union (FSU) need to be viewed with considerable caution. Estimates of Kazakhstan's oil wealth seem to suffer more than most from hyperbole, varying enormously, with the Kazakhs themselves sometimes guilty of

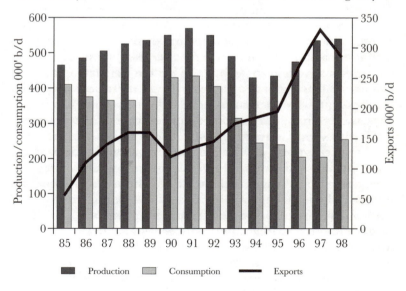

Figure 5.4: Kazakh Crude Oil Production, Consumption and Exports. 1985–98. Thousand Barrels per Day

the wildest exaggeration in their figures. One estimate from the Kazakh Geological Institute in 1994 put potential reserves for the pre-Caspian (i.e. North Caspian) basin alone at 50 billion barrels of crude, 15 billion barrels of condensate, and 8 trillion cubic metres of gas. The optimism as yet remains unjustified by actual discoveries.

The most important Kazakh operated field in recent years has been Mangistau, with a current output of some 80 thousand barrels per day. In the continued absence of a main export route, Kazakh oil exports are destined to develop slowly, in a piecemeal fashion. Indeed, there must now be serious questions as to whether any real volumes to speak of can be expected to reach Mediterranean markets within the time-frame of this study. Kazakh exports have always been heavily reliant on the volume permitted to travel through the Russian Transneft pipeline system.

Despite being the most extensive pipeline system in the world, the Russian network is unsuited to current conditions in that it does not deliver to the major export locations. Instead, most pipelines terminate in areas currently suffering from low demand. Russia still maintains control of most pipelines in the Former Soviet Union, and dictates who transports what in the region, allocating export capacity and delivery schedules. With quota restrictions on volumes shipped to Novorossiysk, alternative outlets have had to be found to enable Tengiz output to be increased. This impetus has given rise to various solutions, such as swap deals with Azerbaijan, Iran, deliveries by rail and inland waterway, resulting in an overall modest growth in net exports.

Direct exports from Kazakhstan began in April 1996, when the Tengizchevroil (TCO) joint venture between Chevron, Mobil and Kazakh Oil opened several routes for its increasing production from Tengiz, including through the Azeri/Georgian corridor. From Tengiz, oil was sent to Aktau, on the east Caspian, then shipped to Azerbaijan, from where it was railed to Batum and loaded onto tankers for delivery into the Mediterranean. Further development of the Tengiz field depends on finding adequate transport routes to carry the crude outside the FSU. Kazakh exports through the Transneft pipeline system are currently restricted to 140 thousand barrels per day. The logjam is intended to be broken by the Caspian Pipeline

Consortium (CPC) pipeline from Tengiz to Novorossiysk. While the subject of numerous delays, the CPC pipeline is intended to have 560 thousand b/d of initial capacity by about 2003, increasing to 1.34 million b/d after 2010.

With the current pipeline system inadequate to transport growing production, and TCO's quota in the pipeline to Samara (where it is blended with Urals and sent to Russian refineries) strictly limited, makeshift solutions have become increasingly important. In an attempt to reduce its reliance on the existing pipeline system, and boost production, TCO has been forced to develop a complex assortment of high cost alternative export routes, especially rail routes, particularly in view of the delays in the CPC pipeline.

In terms of potential supply increments there are three main consortia in Kazakhstan, which we consider in turn. The first is Tengizchevroil, (TCO), led by Chevron, Kazakh Oil and Mobil. Commercial production at the giant Tengiz field in north-west Kazakhstan began in 1991, but was delayed by the collapse of the Soviet Union and a lack of funds. Estimates of recoverable reserves vary considerably between 4 billion and 15 billion barrels of oil, with production so far dictated by Russia's granting access to the Transneft pipeline system.

The joint venture planned to use the Russian pipeline system to export the crude. An agreement was reached in September 1993 to allow for delivery to Novorossiysk, but complications arose due to the problems of the Caspian Pipeline Consortium and there was no early pipeline option available. In 1997, TCO began shipping crude across the Caspian via Azerbaijan to Batum on the Georgian Black Sea, by rail, barge and pipeline. In early 1998, TCO sent a test load of 40,000 barrels to western China by rail, and was also able to increase the volume of its crude to Batum, as new rail loading facilities at Dubendi in Azerbaijan became operational. The export routes currently in use can however be little more than a series of short-term measures incurring heavy rail transport costs of about $6 per barrel.

The second major consortium is Karachaganak, shared between BG, Agip, Texaco, and Lukoil. Average oil production from the giant Karachaganak development was just under 50 thousand b/d in 1997. The signing of a production-sharing contract in November 1997 seemed to herald a turning point for the beleaguered project partners. The first phase of the development envisaged a rise in crude and condensate production to 175 thousand barrels per day by 2001 and a peak of 260 thousand b/d, although the field has been experiencing production problems which may make the original projections look rather optimistic. Reserves at Karachaganak are estimated by Kazakh sources at 1.3 trillion cubic metres of gas, 654 million tonnes of condensate and 189 million tonnes of crude oil, totalling some 6.2 billion barrels of liquids. A probably more realistic and widely accepted figure is 2.4 billion barrels of liquids.

The 120 thousand b/d of capacity owned by Agip and BG in the CPC's Tengiz-Novorossiysk pipeline is likely to be important in terms of the development of the project. Karachaganak condensate is of a similar quality to Tengiz crude, and could be pumped direct to Novorossiysk. This would allow the partners to avoid the major difficulties they have been facing with Gazprom, which has maintained a stranglehold on output from the field. All condensate is currently stabilised and processed at a plant in Orenburg, Russia. Charges for the processing are said to be exorbitant, and output restricted. Mobil's attempts to ship the condensate from the field proved problematic. There is now optimism that any one of many options could open up during the forty-year lifespan of the project, but at the moment the main priority, as with much else in the Kazakh oil and gas industry, is for an accommodation with the Russians. During 1993 and1994, Gazprom held talks with the Kazakhs over the field, and an agreement was signed with the Kazakh Oil and Gas Ministry in December 1996 allowing for Gazprom's participation. However, Gazprom subsequently withdrew from the venture, reportedly due to disagreements with its partners.

The third consortium is known as OKIOC, the Offshore Kazakhstan International Operating Company (previously known as the Caspian Sea Consortium). The composition of the OKIOC group, with one-seventh shares held by Agip, the BP/Statoil alliance, BG, Total, Mobil, Shell and KazakOil. Following the signing of a major production-sharing agreement in Washington in 1997, members of the consortium selected twelve prospective blocks covering 6 thousand square kilometres in the Kazakh sector of the Caspian Sea. Development of the reserves is expected to be a complex and initially costly process, due to difficult geological conditions offshore. Moreover, a lack of infrastructure onshore, coupled with rising sea levels and freezing during the winter months, make this a long-term, risky project, and one prone to production schedule slippage.

A further entry into the sector came in the form of the involvement of the main upstream Chinese state company, CNPC. As part of a flurry of deal making in Iraq, Venezuela and Kazakhstan over the course of 1997, CNPC secured a 60 per cent stake in Aktyubinskneft, (currently producing 50 thousand b/d with reserves of 860 million barrels from its main fields Kenkiyak, Zhanazhol and Alibekmola). CNPC beat Amoco and Texaco to secure the assets, which also include ownership of the Uzen production association. The Uzen field has reserves of over 1.5 billion barrels, making it Kazakhstan's second largest oilfield. The deal included a CNPC option to build a 3000 km pipeline, linking the fields to Xinjiang province in western China, at a cost of $3.5 billion. That project has now been shelved.

Table 5.2 shows a summary of development prospects in Kazakhstan based on optimistic views of output projections being

Table 5.2: Major Oil Prospects in Kazakhstan. Potential Peak Production and Reserves.

Field	Peak Output Thousand b/d	Reserves billion barrels
Development		
Karachaganak	290	1.2
Uzen	50	1.5
Kumkol	50	0.6
Kenkiyak	40	0.3
Tengiz (Main)	400	4.0
Zhanazhol	160	0.8
Kalamkas	80	0.8
Karazhanbas	60	1.0
North Buzachi	50	0.5
Exploration		
North Caspian Basin	740	8–12

fulfilled. Timetables are as prone to slippage in Kazakhstan as in Azerbaijan, but on current information the increase in production is slow, leaving Kazakh production to rise by some 1 million b/d in a decade. Over that time period, the increase represents but a small ripple in the world market.

3.   Iraq

The view that one takes of the impact of Iraq on the oil market over the next decade depends on whose eyes you look through. A geologist or an exploration and development manager would look at the reserve base, and reach a swift diagnosis along the following lines. In all there are 73 known oilfields in Iraq, six of which are classified as supergiants and seventeen as giants. Almost two-thirds of the reserves are in six oilfields, including the supergiants of Kirkuk in the north and Rumaila in the south, which currently dominate Iraqi production. Many significant fields have not yet been developed, including Majnoon (20 billion barrels) and West Qurna (15 billion barrels), Nahr Umr (6 billion barrels) and Halfaya (5 billion barrels). Development and operating costs are low, the terrain relatively undemanding, technical requirements easy to fulfil, and vast tracts of highly prospective areas remain unexplored.

Our geologist would assume that making further major discoveries would be as perplexing a task as shooting fish in a barrel. Our development manager would marvel at 46 billion barrels waiting to be developed in just four fields. Both would conclude that the opening up of Iraq represents the greatest opportunity for decades, and that Iraq would play host to one of the greatest oil booms in history. As for production capacity, they would note that if you produced in Iraq at the same production to reserves ratio as the UK, you would be producing 60 million barrels per day. In other words, they would claim that realistically any target up to 10 million b/d was perfectly feasible.

If we look at the same situation through the eyes of a petroleum engineer or a politician, it would be given a very different gloss. The engineer would note that the damage done over the last eighteen years (through eight years of wars and eight years of sanctions), goes beyond the impact on the infrastructure of exports, the gathering stations, ports and pipelines. It also extends to the operating fields themselves. Iraq has shown that even a high pressure, well behaved, Middle East supergiant oilfield can be severely damaged through lack of use and failure of maintenance. Neither Kirkuk nor Rumaila are the fields they once were, and the spectre of water coning has become reality. The politician would note that the time line to any form of normalisation with Iraq is potentially a very long one, and there is far more to the route than the simple question of when sanctions will be lifted.

We have tended towards the second interpretation. With a swift lifting of the sanctions regime, an Iraq unconstrained in capital markets and having international goodwill in reconstruction, and with a swift technical fix to the current problems, a fast take-off of Iraqi production becomes a possibility. The chance that all four of these conditions will be met is exceedingly remote, and quite plausibly none of them may hold.

In 1979, prior to the Iran–Iraq War, crude oil production peaked at an average of 3.5 million b/d, while production capacity had risen to 3.8 million barrels per day. The Iran–Iraq War significantly reduced production and impeded further development. The Gulf terminals, along with storage facilities were destroyed, and the planned development of undeveloped supergiant fields was halted. However, after the initial severe fall from 3.5 million b/d to 0.9 million b/d between 1979 and 1981, production climbed throughout the war. Immediately prior to Iraq's invasion of Kuwait on 2 August 1990, exports had climbed to 2.8 million b/d, of which 1.6 mb/d was shipped to the Mediterranean through the Kirkuk-Ceyhan pipeline to Turkey, 0.8 mb/d via the IPSA2 pipeline across Saudi Arabia to the Red Sea (where it was possible to ship to the Mediterranean through the Suez Canal or Sumed pipeline), 0.3 mb/d from the Mina al-Bakr terminal on the Gulf, and just below 0.1 mb/d exported by truck.

In July 1990, Iraq's hand was a strong one, and a discernible power shift was taking place within OPEC. Counterfactual history is not a useful device, but it is perhaps worth noting the plausibility of the following scenario had the invasion of Kuwait not taken place. By 1998, Saudi Arabia would not be producing in excess of 8 million b/d, and Iraq quite conceivably would have reached 6 million barrels per day. The balance of power would have been very different. In all, Iraq's timing was the worst possible. Had the invasion been earlier, then Cold War politics would have prevented the liberation of Kuwait. Had Iraq waited, then many of the Iraqi objectives could have been met by non-military means.

In the counterfactual history, a rise of Iraqi production from some 3.2 million b/d in July 1990 to 6 million b/d in 1998 seems possible, but still perhaps unlikely. Yet often bullish cases for the recovery of Iraq project larger increases in a shorter time period. Further, the conditions of 2000 are very different from 1990, in terms of the infrastructure available, access to capital markets and the general state of the economy. Until the full lifting of sanctions occurs and there is a clarification of the post sanctions position, Iraq is not even at a standing start let alone the running start it had in 1990.

While perhaps the major short-term problems lie with production constraints, it is worth beginning with the longer lasting export capacity constraints. The key point is that the 1.65 million b/d Petroline pipeline through Saudi Arabia for loading on the Red Sea at Yanbu for all practical purposes no longer exists as even a long-term option. It thus joins the Banias line to Syria, the Haifa line to Israel and the Tripoli line to Lebanon on the list of Iraq's lost pipelines. Iraq is left with Mina al-Bakr, the Ceyhan pipeline, the hope of reactivated access through Syria, and the extremely limited possibilities of moving oil by truck.

In the short to medium term, shipments into the Mediterranean will be constrained by the operating capacity of the Ceyhan pipeline, as shown in Figure 5.5. This covers over 1000 kilometres and links Iraq's Kirkuk oilfield to the port of Ceyhan on Turkey's Mediterranean coast. The pipeline was opened in 1977 with an initial capacity of 0.5 million b/d, rising to 0.7 in 1978 and 1 million b/d in 1984. Debottlenecking work led to a further expansion to 1.1 million barrels per day. A second parallel pipeline with a capacity of 0.5 million b/d was opened in 1987, designed to carry Basrah Light crude. The imposition of the UN embargo in August 1990 led to the shutting down of the pipelines, which remained closed until 1997 and the start of

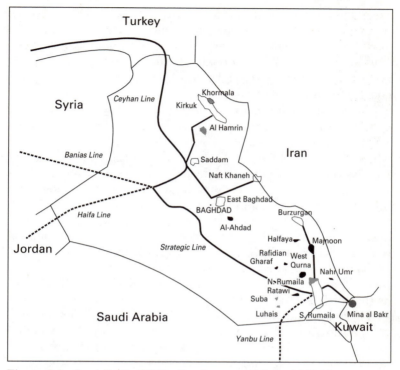

Figure 5.5: Iraqi Crude Oil Pipeline System and Selected Fields

the first oil for food deal between Iraq and the UN. At that time capacity was constrained at 0.8 million b/d in the absence of full operability of a crucial pumping station. With the continuation of repairs, capacity has been eased up by stages back towards the full 1.6 million b/d capacity.

The Strategic Pipeline, also shown in Figure 5.5, was built during the 1970s to link Iraq's northern and southern pipelines. It provides some flexibility as to choice of export routes enabling, if necessary, oil from the southern fields to be shipped out through Turkey, while Kirkuk oil could be shipped through the Gulf. This 46 inch pipeline with a capacity of 1.4 million b/d could be used to ship out Basrah Light via Ceyhan, using a repaired Haditha pipeline for storage and batching purposes. However, until sanctions are lifted, the volume and direction of shipments would also be affected by the UN resolutions which specify that 60 per cent of Iraq's petroleum exports should leave the country via Turkey. Hence the capacity constraint to Ceyhan also constrains Mina al-Bakr exports. In total, before even considering the poor state of oilfield production facilities, exports are severely impacted on by logistical bottlenecks and UN constraints on egress points.

The production facilities themselves are a further cause for extreme bearishness about Iraq's production prospects. In March 1998 a UN Group of Experts (GoE) visited Iraq to try to establish whether Iraq could meet the level of exports permitted under Resolution 1153. Their overall general impression was one of a severe deterioration in production facilities and in the logistical infrastructure of the oil industry. The problem is essentially one of severe reservoir damage, loss of pressure and water coning, and the impact of years of poor maintenance given the lack of spare parts. The bullish case for Iraqi recovery uses the recovery of Kuwait as a parallel. In reality, Russia provides a better parallel, and the recovery of Iraqi production might be as slow as that of Russian.

There are concerns that oil quality may have been affected during sanctions. This has arisen not only from the destruction of wet oil treatment facilities and the shortage of chemicals but also because of the injection of surplus fuel oil into the wells. Some 150 thousand b/d of surplus fuel oil have been injected into the Kirkuk field over a prolonged period, a useful short-term fix for getting rid of it, but with unknown and potentially unfortunate longer-term consequences for the reservoir. Water logging is the most immediate problem, and it is severely restricting production at both the Kirkuk and South Rumaila fields.

Without rapid and sizeable investments it will be difficult, if not impossible, to counteract the declining production curve in the existing reservoirs. The longer the proposed investment is delayed then the wider will be the gap between the existing decline curve and the projected increase in production. In addition to finance, there is a need for expertise to implement the proposed improvements and some expertise and technical knowledge (few pre-1990 Iraqi technicians are left in the industry), will be required to gradually raise production over the next few years. Returning Iraq to pre-sanctions capacity levels then not only requires the transportation logistics problems to be solved, it also needs the development of new fields as existing fields have a permanently reduced capacity.

The development of new fields brings us to the question of foreign participation. During the late 1980s plans were presented and partly implemented to raise production capacity, and Iraq opened discussions with foreign companies to develop super giant fields with the then aim of raising productive capacity to 6 million b/d. The current process is to a large extent a reopening of the old negotiations, and the 6 million b/d target is back, this time at the end of a ten-year timeline from the ending of sanctions.

The stated objective of the Iraqi government is to raise $30 billion of investment in the upstream oil and gas sector in order to increase production to the target within a decade of the ending of sanctions. There are three prongs to the Iraqi strategy. First, to raise production from existing fields to the pre-war level of 3.5 million b/d; this would be achieved by using $210 million of oil revenues to purchase spare parts and equipment and through the assistance of foreign technology and financing. We have already suggested however that 3.5 million b/d may be impossible from current fields simply by acquiring spare parts. To restore those fields would probably need a complete re-engineering or brown field development. Secondly, Iraq wishes to develop new oil fields through signing production-sharing agreements (PSAs) and service contracts in order to expand sustainable production by at least 2.5 million barrels per day. Finally, they wish to negotiate risk contracts with foreign companies to explore and develop certain blocks in the Western Desert.

More than twenty companies have initialled preliminary contracts for oil exploration and development when sanctions are lifted. Foreign companies are involved in three forms of contracts. First, there are engineering and service contracts to maintain and expand existing capacity. In these, the foreign company finances and recovers costs and additional reward from the oil produced, has no rights to the oil but may have the option to purchase the oil. Secondly, there are PSAs for the development of at least ten giant and super giant fields. In these contracts the company finances the project and recovers costs and additional rewards through sharing the oil produced.

While based on the traditional PSAs, the fact that these fields have been appraised and are ready for development has led to specific clauses being incorporated into the agreements. An Iraqi organisation, designated by the Ministry, is to have a 25 per cent participation in the contract. Part of the costs of this participation is borne by the existing asset and some may be met by the foreign partner. Finally, there are the exploration risk contracts to develop nine Western Desert blocks. The contractual terms for these are similar to the traditional PSAs, with an entitlement to develop any fields discovered while investment and rewards are met through shares of cost and profit oil. The exploration period is fixed at five years with a possible extension for a further two years.

The PSAs and buyback deals under discussion or signed are shown in Table 5.3. The fields involved were shown in Figure 5.5, with the PSA fields shown in black and the buyback fields shown in grey. The key element in the geography of the deals is that they are mainly in South Iraq. Even in the extremely unlikely event of a very swift increase in production arising from PSAs and buyback deals, the natural development and capacity expansion in infrastructure would be towards Mina al Bakr and not towards Ceyhan. The only deals that would naturally tie in with the northern system are the buyback deals for Khormala and Al Hamrin, amounting to some 180 thousand b/d of incremental production, and the PSA signed for Al-Ahdad. As the latter is being developed with Chinese capital, the natural preference for egress would be through Mina al Bakr.

In total, of the highly optimistic 3.7 million b/d increment shown in Table 5.3, over 3.5 million b/d would leave Iraq through Mina al Bakr should logistics allow. We then see no likelihood of any rush of Iraqi oil into the Mediterranean for two reasons. First, we doubt that incremental production will come on stream quickly or smoothly, and secondly that even if it did, it would not enter the world market via Ceyhan. As far as direct Iraqi loadings in the Mediterranean are concerned, the recovered capacity of the routes to Ceyhan of 1.6 million b/d would then be the limit. Southern oil might occasionally go north via the strategic line if there were line fill problems on the Ceyhan route. However, unless export capacity expansion

Table 5.3:   Prospective Foreign Investment Contracts in Iraq as of 2000

a) Production-Sharing Agreements

Field	Estimated Capacity thousand b/d	Oil Gravity	Estimated Cost US$ m	Bidders
Al-Ahdad	90	24–7	700	CNPC-Norinco
West Qurna (Phase 2[1])	600	27, 37	3700	Lukoil led consortium
Majnoon	600	28, 35	3,000–4,000	Elf
Nahr Umr	440	22, 32, 42	3400	Total
Nassiryah	300	26, 38	1900	ENI, Repsol
Halfaya	225	23, 31	2000	BHP, CNPC, Korean consortium
Ratawi	200	20–26, 39	1300	Petronas, Crescent, Shell, Can Oxy
Tuba	180	24, 28	500	ONGC, Pertamina, Sonatrach
Gharaf	100	21–25, 35–37	500	TPAO, Japex
Rafidain	100	25, 40	500	Perenco, Sidanco
Total	2835		18000	

b) Buy-Back Deals

Field	Estimated Capacity thousand b/d	Oil Gravity	Estimated Cost US$ m	Bidders
North Rumalia 4th Payzone Lukoil, Zarubezhnelt	500	26	-	Mashinoimport, Taftneft,
Khormala	100	36	-	Petrom
Al Hamrin	80	28–29	-	Stroyexport, IPC
Suba	50	27–32	100	Mashinoexport, Larmag
Luhais	30	30, 27	100	Lormag, Mashinoimport
Total	760		-	

Sources: Energy Intelligence Group, *Middle East Economic Survey*, Morgan Stanley, *OPEC Bulletin*

in the Gulf hit an absolutely unbreechable constraint, there would be little reason to add to Ceyhan capacity because of the new production capacity coming on stream in the south.

The PSAs that have been signed should perhaps be treated more as statements of intent, as it seems unlikely that the unconstraining of Iraq will be a process that will not warrant renegotiations. However, for what the contracts are worth, the first PSA was signed in March 1997, with a consortium headed by Russia's Lukoil involved in a 23-year, $3.7 billion oil deal to develop 8 billion barrels in the West Qurna oilfield. A second PSA was signed three months later with the Chinese National Petroleum Corporation and partners to develop the Al-Ahdad field at a projected cost of $700 million. The PSAs with the Russians and Chinese involve the establishment of a contractor group owned jointly by the foreign partners (75 per cent) and an Iraqi organisation (25 per cent). The contractor would be responsible for all the development costs which would be recouped as cost oil from production. The remaining output would be profit oil divided between the government and the contractor group. Elf and Total have been conducting negotiations for PSAs for the super giant fields of Nahr Umr and Majnoon respectively. The former has a projected cost of $3.4 billion and an estimated production capacity of 440 thousand b/d from reserves of 7 billion barrels. The latter, costing $3–4 billion has a production capacity of 600 thousand barrels per day. As is shown in Table 5.3, other companies have held detailed negotiations with Iraq but the arrangements have so far fallen short of actual contracts. In addition, in late 1997, Iraq invited international partners to invest in natural gas projects worth over $4 billion.

The deals with foreign capital can eventually increase production sharply; in the case of the development deals there is after all no exploration risk and the reservoirs would be the largest new developments in the world over the last thirty years. However, it would be wrong to think that Iraq is on the fast track to dramatically increased production. First, the development lags would in themselves be long, even without other constraints. Secondly, the transportation infrastructure would need considerable additions, again involving lags and the need to source materials. Thirdly, even when sanctions are lifted, Iraq is not necessarily likely to have easy access to capital or the enthusiastic support of the US government. As Libya's experience has shown, the lifting of UN sanctions can merely mean that the constraints take another, but none the less still binding form.

Notes

1. Richard Morningstar, testimony to Senate International Economic Policy, Export and Trade Promotion Subcommittee Hearing, 3 March, 1999.
2. Quoted in *Oil and Gas Journal*, 27 September 1999.

6 THE MEDITERRANEAN OIL MARKET

1. Introduction

The Mediterranean market complex hardly exists as an independent entity relative to the highly developed markets in northern Europe and the USA. There is no price leader among indigenous crude oils, and in oil products the size of the market is swamped in terms of volume and influence by the Rotterdam market. The only crude oil price that has any claim to being representative of Mediterranean conditions is Russian Urals, a heavy and sour crude priced on a delivered basis, while the bulk of Mediterranean production is very light and sweet and priced on a f.o.b. basis. Given that Urals is all there is, the differential between Brent and Urals is then of interest, even if dominated in price formation by the quality differences between the crudes and the erratic nature of Urals and Iraqi deliveries into the eastern Mediterranean. In the next section we attempt to explain this differential, and to derive from it a measure for the competitiveness of North Sea and West African crude oil in the Mediterranean market place.

An active spot market is a fundamental condition for the development of any market complex, and any price leadership role. In Section 3 we detail the evolution of the Mediterranean market, with its structural shifts and low component of indigenous Mediterranean crude oils. A final section provides some conclusions for the study as a whole.

2. The Brent-Urals Differential

The analysis of the differential between dated Brent and Urals provides us with some indicators about the dynamics of the regional market. A distinction has sometimes been drawn between the eastern Mediterranean as an area of Urals dominance, and the western Mediterranean where Brent and other North Sea or West African crude oils can gain greater penetration. That is somewhat misleading, as many Mediterranean refiners tend to be active blenders, changing the relative split of their crude oil slate between heavy and light oils

120

according to market conditions. Indeed, as refinery complexity tends to increase as one moves east to west on the European side of the Mediterranean, the more natural market for the Urals, subject to price differentials, is often in the eastern Mediterranean.

There is however a strong interplay between Brent and Urals, and this section seeks to address the question as to how the nature of this relationship has evolved and exactly where Brent and Urals are being arbitraged. In particular, we wish to derive an indicator to determine those periods in which Brent and Brent-related North Sea and West African crude oil are being pulled further into the Mediterranean, and those periods when they are being forced out. With the complications added by the time structure of prices and by freight rates, combined with the uncertainty over precisely where the pricing axis is located, the simple Brent-Urals price differential is unable to serve as this indicator. Our alternative indicator is outlined below.

Considering first the historical pattern, the differential between the price of dated Brent and Urals is shown as a monthly average in Figure 6.1, together with the difference in their gross product worths evaluated with f.o.b. Mediterranean prices. All prices are drawn from those assessed by *Platt's Oilgram*,

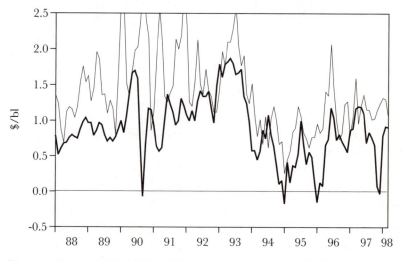

Figure 6.1: Brent–Urals Price Differential (broad) and GPW Difference (narrow). 1988–98. Dollars per Barrel

i.e. the Urals price is assessed c.i.f. Augusta in Sicily, while the Brent price is assessed f.o.b. at Sullom Voe. As well as considerable volatility, the path of the differential has shown a major discontinuity. From 1988 through to early 1993, there was a clear upwards trend, with, on yearly averages, Brent's premium over Urals increasing by about 15 cents each year. In early 1993 the average peaked at about $1.80 per barrel, before entering into severe decline over the following two years. In January 1995, Urals moved temporarily to a premium over Brent, and following this the differential has remained bounded between a low of rough parity, and a high of $1.20 per barrel.

The strong downwards movement that started in 1993 and has not been corrected since, was primarily a feature of global trends. An expansion of cracking capacity, particularly in northern Europe, was based on the assumption that light to heavy crude oil differentials would continue to increase in perpetuity. The raft of new crackers then biased the marginal crude oil demand towards heavy oil. However, the marginal crude oil supply has instead become more biased towards lighter oil, driven primarily by the surge in North Sea output, reinforced by the actions of a volume constrained Saudi Arabia in shutting in Arab Heavy in order to increase production of its lighter grades. The factors behind the 1993 slide in differentials have still to work their way out of the system, heavy to light differentials remain low and the overhang of cracking capacity is still manifest in the northern European gasoline surplus. While final product demand has been becoming lighter and requires a lower sulphur content, the combined effect of changes in refinery configurations and in crude oil production quality have continued to at least keep pace. The need for differentials to widen out again since 1993 has thus so far been obviated.

While there is a clear relationship between relative gross product worths and the price differential, as seen in Figure 6.1, there is also a strong explanatory role for the time structure of prices. The standard cargo represented by the Platt's Urals quote is, at the time of a deal being transacted, closer to market in the Mediterranean than is Brent. Backwardations in prices then disadvantage Brent, and will drive down the Brent-Urals differential. Note how in Figure 6.1, the first three of the four periods when the monthly average differential has become negative have coincided with periods of sharp backwardation. Likewise, in times of contango, to remain competitive the Urals price is depressed relative to Brent.

We then need a method for incorporating the time structure with its correct weighting, as well as making an allowance for the difference between the f.o.b. basis of the Brent price and the c.i.f. basis of the Urals price. We have adopted the following procedure. We have taken the difference between the two series shown in Figure 6.1, i.e. the GPW difference minus the price differential. We have then regressed the level of North Europe to Mediterranean and the level of one month's time structure of prices, forcing the intercept through zero.

The coefficient of most interest is that on the freight rate. That coefficient, call it β, provides an indication, albeit not necessarily an immediately intuitive one, of what has been the average point of Urals and Brent arbitrage. The interpretation of β is as follows. Arbitrage between Urals and Brent takes place at a point where the ratio of the freight cost from Sullom Voe to the *incremental* freight cost of a Urals cargo moving further east than Augusta is given by the expression $(1 + \beta)/(1 - \beta)$. Hence, were the coefficient to be -1, then we would have the rather unlikely case that Brent and Urals were arbitraged at Sullom Voe. At the other extreme, were the coefficient to be $+1$, then the point of arbitrage would be at Augusta.

The coefficient estimated from the regression was 0.64, with a very low standard error. From the above, the interpretation of this is that the pricing axis has normally occurred where the ratio of the Brent freight to the incremental freight from Augusta is about five. This would be broadly consistent with south France, and for the purposes of the exposition below we have assumed the pricing axis to be Lavera.

Plotting the monthly average of the differentials from our estimated regression results in the series shown in Figure 6.2, with a twelve-month average superimposed for clarity. The interpretation of this series is that whenever it is negative the pricing axis has moved to the west of Lavera, i.e. the penetration of Brent into the Mediterranean has been reduced, and vice versa for a positive value. An alternative, but equivalent, explanation is that the series shows what would be the per barrel advantage in purchasing Brent compared to Urals for a fully

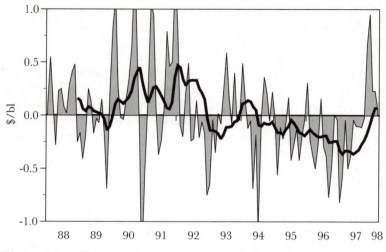

Figure 6.2:   Differentials from Brent–Urals Arbitrage at Lavera. 1988–98.
Dollars per Barrel

flexible refinery at Lavera. This opportunity is defined in terms
of a decision to purchase either a dated Brent cargo or spot
Urals, not only considering gross product worths but also fully
taking the correct weighting of the time structure of prices and
freight rates into account.

A feature of Figure 6.2 is the high of level of volatility, with
the relative position of the crude oils prone to occasional sharp
movements. However, it also shows that an advantage is often
slow to erode, with the series normally staying positive or
negative for several successive months. There is also a distinct
pattern across time. The penetration that Brent, and, more
generally, non-Mediterranean light crude oil was able to achieve
in the early 1990s has been eroded. After 1992, the series has
normally been negative, and the yearly average trended down
fairly consistently until the end of 1997.

The rolling average series shown in Figure 6.2, eventually
turns back up at the end of 1997, and implies that Brent briefly
achieved more penetration into the Mediterranean than it had
for six years. The market circumstances at this time represented
the best possible combination for moving oil into the
Mediterranean. The world market as a whole was weak, and a
contango in prices had opened up, reducing the relative

disadvantage of longer haul oil. At the same time, the eastern Mediterranean market was tight, primarily due to a hiatus in Iraqi exports, and so the Brent-Urals spread was collapsing.

3. Spot Crude Oil Markets

The current nature of price formation and crude oil trading in the Mediterranean is perhaps best encapsulated by the answer to the question of when was a deal last transacted in flat price terms in the area and reported to a price assessment agency. The answer is 1990. The vacuum seems even greater when one learns that the cargo concerned contained the rather esoteric Italian grade Raspo, and perhaps unsurprisingly was the only ever reported spot deal for the grade. Raspo is not a crude that would be an obvious candidate for a price leader role, and one suspects that coming to a flat price agreement was probably just as easy as sorting out the correct differential (it was settled at the equivalent of dated Brent minus $5.92).

The general characterisation of the market is that it is thin and trades solely in differentials from the established marker crude oils. While in 1987 flat price spot deals for Mediterranean crude oil were reported at the rate of one per trading day, in the 1990s the market has been almost exclusively dated Brent related. The spot market remains extremely limited in size. In Table 6.1 we show the total number of spot deals reported to the price assessment agency Petroleum Argus from 1986 to 1997, for the North Sea, West Africa and the Mediterranean.

As shown in Table 6.1, the Mediterranean market in spot crude oil has reported a steady level of about seven deals per week since 1994, and, as of 1997, is more liquid than that for West African oil. However, it remains dwarfed by the North Sea market, and, as noted above, throughout the 1990s has provided nothing but differential price information. It has also, for reasons discussed further below, contracted from its peak size of 1992 and 1993. The size of the information set generated in the Mediterranean is therefore small, and of course it shrinks into complete insignificance when we add to the North Sea spot market the far greater volume of information generated by the Brent complex of forward, futures and CFDs.

The pattern shown in Table 6.1 of rising spot market volumes

Table 6.1: Reported Spot Deals by Region. 1986–97.

	North Sea	West Africa	Mediterranean
1986	928	186	181
1987	872	353	284
1988	1,102	275	226
1989	1,069	494	248
1990	1,087	606	266
1991	1,634	780	345
1992	1,806	843	546
1993	1,876	788	614
1994	1,587	614	391
1995	1,542	491	391
1996	1,612	451	377
1997	1,480	252	382

Source: Own Calculations from Petroleum Argus Crude Oil Deals Database.

until 1993, followed by a retrenchment and stability thereafter, is rather misleading in its implication of some coherence and gentle evolution in the pattern of trade. Underlying these figures is far greater turbulence in the nature of the market and in the composition of what is traded. This is illustrated in Table 6.2, which shows the breakdown of trade in the Mediterranean by the country of origin of the crude oil.[1]

Table 6.2: Spot Crude Oil Deals in the Mediterranean by Country of Crude Origin. 1986–97. Number of Reported Deals.

	86	87	88	89	90	91	92	93	94	95	96	97
Algeria	30	50	40	40	34	39	60	36	22	19	17	26
Egypt	97	69	59	37	30	38	54	29	40	25	13	16
Iran	24	72	46	84	107	119	168	222	65	46	38	14
Kazakhstan	-	-	-	-	-	-	-	-	-	-	3	14
Libya	17	60	48	38	36	19	9	7	9	1	2	-
Morocco	-	-	-	-	-	9	11	2	2	1	1	-
Russia	8	32	29	30	39	76	200	257	224	261	274	282
Syria	5	-	2	14	13	35	40	58	34	35	25	28
Tunisia	-	1	2	5	6	10	3	3	1	3	4	2
Italy/Spain	-	-	-	-	1	-	1	-	-	-	-	-
TOTAL	181	284	226	248	266	345	546	614	391	391	377	382

Source: Own Calculations from Petroleum Argus Crude Oil Deals Database

Table 6.2 shows some strong structural shifts in the market over the last decade, and a distinct difference between light and heavy oil. Trade in the output of the Mediterranean light crude producers is as of 1997 insignificant. In 1987, there were 179 deals in the combined output of Algeria, Libya, and Egypt, but by 1997 this had shrunk to an annual rate of forty. Spot trade in Libyan oil is now all but extinct, and Algerian spot crude oil deals (including that loaded through the Tunisian port of La Skhirra) amount to just one deal a fortnight. In the severely truncated light sweet spot market, the most active market is now that for Syrian oil, followed by Algerian (54 deals in 1997 between the two countries). Yet the two light sweet Mediterranean grades that *Platt's Oilgram* currently assess are from Libya and Egypt (just sixteen deals in Egyptian oil and none in Libyan). There is a certain peculiarity about the situation where an American agency is assessing the spot market in a Libyan oil which no American company can buy, and in which there is today no spot market in any case. We would then suggest that there is a strong indication that what is structurally a thin market, is also being badly served by current price assessment. Within such a thin market, to then complicate matters by assessing a grade where there is no trade is somewhat bizarre.

The most striking features of Table 6.2 are the time paths in trade of Russian and Iranian grades. To consider Iranian spot trade first, an active market in the Mediterranean for loadings out of Sidi Kerir has fallen away sharply in recent years, to reach its current level of little more than one reported deal per month. There are several factors behind this. The first is simply that there is now far less Iranian oil available. The rise in consumption since 1992 relative to production is enough in itself to account for the disappearance per year of over 300 Iranian spot and term cargoes. Added to this has been a general marketing shift away from the Mediterranean and into Asia, with the proportion of total Iranian crude oil exports heading east now above 40 per cent compared to a level of below 30 per cent at the start of the decade.

A third factor has been the impact of US sanctions on Iran, particularly the prohibition on US firms running Iranian crude oil through any of their refineries, including those outside of the USA itself. While this has of course cut down the number of refineries in Europe able to run Iranian crude oil and thus made spot sales a little more difficult, its major impact has been more due to political symbolism. This has created a strong political imperative for Iran to avoid the appearance of any overt excess supply of Iranian oil, i.e. to favour term sales over spot to cut down on the chances of highly visible distressed spot Iranian cargoes in the Mediterranean. (A similar process is also a major factor in the fall in Libyan spot oil trade as shown in Table 6.2). In the early 1990s, the more than occasional appearance of queues of tankers of unsold Iranian spot crude oil was not uncommon. Iranian spot deals were acting as the heavy crude oil swing into the area (with often several additional cargoes beyond that needed for swing), and an unsold cargo waiting for buyers did not carry the same political imagery as it would now. Adding all these factors together, the spot market for Iranian crude oil has been severely squeezed from three directions. There is less oil for export, more of that is going to Asia, and more of what is left is being sold term. In combination, these effects have produced the fall shown in Table 6.2 from 222 spot deals in 1993, to an annual rate of just fourteen in 1997.

The figures in Table 6.2 demonstrate that the Mediterranean spot market is now primarily a market for Russian oil, the proportion of Russian cargoes among total spot deals having increased from less than 5 per cent in 1986 to about 75 per cent in 1997. The reason for the surge in Russian spot availabilities is of course the collapse of the Soviet Union. Due to the continuing battles and the blurring of lines between central authorities and individual regions and enterprises for control of exports, sales have become more fragmented. Before the collapse the export system was based on large deals to oil majors and to western refiners. These companies are still key purchasers of Russian crude, though now by a considerably more circuitous route. Exxon is now the largest lifter of Russian crude, its desire to buy both Urals and Siberian light reinforced by the sanctions enforced loss of the opportunity to run Iranian crude.

We have defined the Mediterranean market for Russian oil to consist of solely those cargoes that load at the Black Sea ports of Odessa, Novorossiysk and Tuapse. Table 6.3 provides the breakdown of total FSU exports by export route, showing

Table 6.3: FSU Exports by Export Route. 1995–99. Million Barrels per Day.

	95	*96*	*97*	*98*	*99*
Black Sea	0.98	1.14	1.19	1.31	1.49
Baltic	0.61	0.77	0.90	0.96	1.01
Total Seaborne	1.59	1.91	2.09	2.27	2.50
Druzhba Pipeline	0.83	0.87	0.84	0.99	1.02
Total Exports	2.42	2.78	2.92	3.30	3.56
Net FSU Exports	2.37	2.72	2.86	3.22	3.53
of which					
Crude Oil	*1.91*	*2.12*	*2.14*	*2.44*	2.62
Oil Products	*0.46*	*0.61*	*0.73*	*0.78*	0.91

Source: IEA *Monthly Oil Market Report*, various issues

that our definition encompasses some 1.5 million barrels per day.

Within the three ports, most shipments to Odessa are absorbed within the area, leaving Novorossiysk and Tuapse as the main outlets for broader international trade. Beyond market structure, there is also the question of the impact of the variability of Urals loadings. Under the Soviet Union, this variability was straightforward seasonality due to the diversion of crude to the domestic market in winter. That centrally planned deliberate seasonal diversion is no longer evident, what we now have is strong variability caused by dislocation, and weather. The large number of exporters causes delays in loading schedules, and general dislocations mean that Urals availability tends always to be either famine or feast. When the variance of Iraqi sales due to loading problems, or more importantly politics, is added to this, we have the effect of large swings in supply occurring independent of any changes in demand conditions.

The composition of buyers and sellers in the Russian spot crude oil trade out of the Black Sea is shown in Table 6.4. The supply side is remarkably fragmented between Russian associations and western traders (adding to the logistical difficulties that have been experienced in the theoretically simple operation of following a loading schedule). Indeed, there is no other non-US crude oil (including all those in the North Sea) that has less concentration among sellers. The buying side of

Table 6.4: Market Shares by Buyer and Seller of Russian Urals into the
Mediterranean. January 1996 to June 1997. Per Cent.

(a) Buyers		*(b) Sellers*	
Company	*Per Cent of Deals*	*Company*	*Per Cent of Deals*
Exxon	14.6	Taurus	15.8
BP	11.6	Nafta	12.9
Shell	10.9	Naftex	8.5
Agip	9.5	Runicom	8.0
Glencore	7.0	Elf	6.8
Repsol	3.9	Petraco	4.4
CFP Total	3.9	Glencore	3.6
Phibro	3.9	Phibro	3.6
Elf	3.4	Lukoil	2.9
OMV	2.8	Sintez	2.9

Source: Own calculations from Petroleum Argus Crude Oil Deals Database

the market is in large part a roll call of exactly the same
companies who constituted the buyers under the Soviet system
of marketing Urals.

4.   The Mediterranean and the World Petroleum Market

The Mediterranean is neither a large producing area, nor a
large consuming area, and it is sandwiched between the
overbearing influence of the huge markets of northern Europe,
Russia and the Middle East. Nevertheless, it plays a role which
arises out of its geographic position; it is a major part of the
linkages between the other centres which constitute the world
petroleum market.

If something changes in the Mediterranean, it almost always
has an external effect as regional supply is static and demand
growth is small in absolute terms. As the Mediterranean alone
is usually unable to absorb an external shock, its effect is
automatically transmitted through to other regions. There is
little direct interaction, for instance, between fluctuations in Iraq
on the one hand, and the North Sea or West Africa on the
other. What provides the conduction between them is the nature
of the Mediterranean, in that a shock produced at one end of

the region is immediately transmitted with an undiluted severity to the other end. For example, fluctuations in Iraqi supply are met barrel by barrel by changes in the outflow of oil through the Straits of Gibraltar. Given this property of transference, the Mediterranean in effect acts as an extension of the Atlantic basin crude oil market, and is the direct interface of that market with the Middle East.

We have found that the scale of variations within the region is small relative to the external variations that feed into the region. In tracking production within the region, we began with an observation of a static profile. Considering the individual countries within the region we found some relatively minor prospective gains in two countries, offset by losses in others. While the 1990s was a decade where emphasis was laid on the impact of technology, and the creep of non-OPEC production as it scaled ever higher peaks, the Mediterranean remained quiet. Only Libya stands out as a producer with the potential to return to the world class of significance within the market, and, despite the removal of UN sanctions, Libya remains to some extent constrained.

The continuing US sanctions on Libya are part of a wider phenomenon within the Mediterranean. Compared to other major crude oil markets, it is by far and away the most distorted by restraints on international trade. All three of the countries facing UN or unilateral US sanctions, i.e. Libya, Iran and Iraq, play an important role within the regional market. Nowhere else in the world is crude oil supply further from any ideal of frictionless trade driven by the market mechanism alone. Politics and politicians impinge heavily on supply, and in affecting trade regimes and also product specifications they also play a dominant role on the demand side.

Turning to the proximate suppliers to the region, we found no basis for some of the wilder claims about the significance of the Caspian, nor about the speed and severity of the impact of the opening up of the Iraqi oil industry. While we would tend to deflate perceptions of the potential scale of expansion of the flows from these areas into the Mediterranean, those flows are still considerable in the regional context. Within the context of the world market, the growth in Caspian production over the next decade hardly registers as an effect. However, within the region the Caspian represents adding the equivalent of another Libya into a regional flow where the domestic producers have a flat production profile. Likewise, the ramping up of export capacity for Iraqi crude oil out of Ceyhan has added large discrete increases in flows in a very short time period. The impact is the same as dropping a large stone into a small puddle.

We found that the Mediterranean has unique characteristics, and unique problems in the downstream of the oil industry. There are major structural deficiencies in the refining industry, in particular a shortage of bottom of the barrel conversion relative to the crude oil input slate, a severe deficiency in desulphurisation capacity. As we saw in the consideration of trade flows, these deficiencies create their own trade patterns for both crude oil and oil products, resulting in a total for trade in and out of the region that far exceeds the notional level of the oil deficit. With the harmonisation of European standards for oil products, a motive force has been created for a convergence in the conditions of refining in northern and Mediterranean Europe. That convergence is not an easy one for regional refiners, and removal of the dislocations implies a period of long and potentially traumatic industrial transition.

On the demand side of the industry, we found that the path of change was not one that would ease the existing dislocations within the refining industry, but instead would exacerbate them. We concentrated on three main issues, heavy fuel oil, product specifications and transportation fuels. The Mediterranean market represents one of the few remaining markets for oil in power generation. We suggested that it has only been with the development of energy infrastructure in the 1990s, that many important countries in the region have been able to make the substitution away from fuel oil that occurred two decades earlier in the USA and northern Europe. That transition is now underway, and means that the common refinery set up in the region of simple but large capacity refineries is no longer appropriate. The change is being driven primarily by Italy. Structural change in the Italian electricity sector, the privatisation and commercialisation of the state electricity generator, and the EU electricity directive, have all combined to provide an extremely strong impetus away from fuel oil.

To date, the quality of oil products in the Mediterranean has been inferior to that in northern Europe, providing a further basis for the structural differences in oil refining. To some extent, the Mediterranean served as a 'quality pit' for dumping lower quality material, in much the same way as we noted that Asia had become a 'quality pit' for high sulphur Mediterranean gasoil. There is now a convergence of standards within Europe, a convergence to a much more rigorous set of standards. As the Mediterranean is starting from a much lower base, the investment demands are far more onerous. An already dislocated sector is becoming even less adequate relative to the requirements placed on it by both the evolution of legislation and by the evolution in the patterns of final consumer demand.

Note

1. As Table 6.2 only shows trade in the Mediterranean, it does not show the full extent of spot trade in Russian crude oil.

INDEX

134